LEADERS OF THE SCIENTIFIC REVOLUTION™

NICOLAUS COPERNICUS

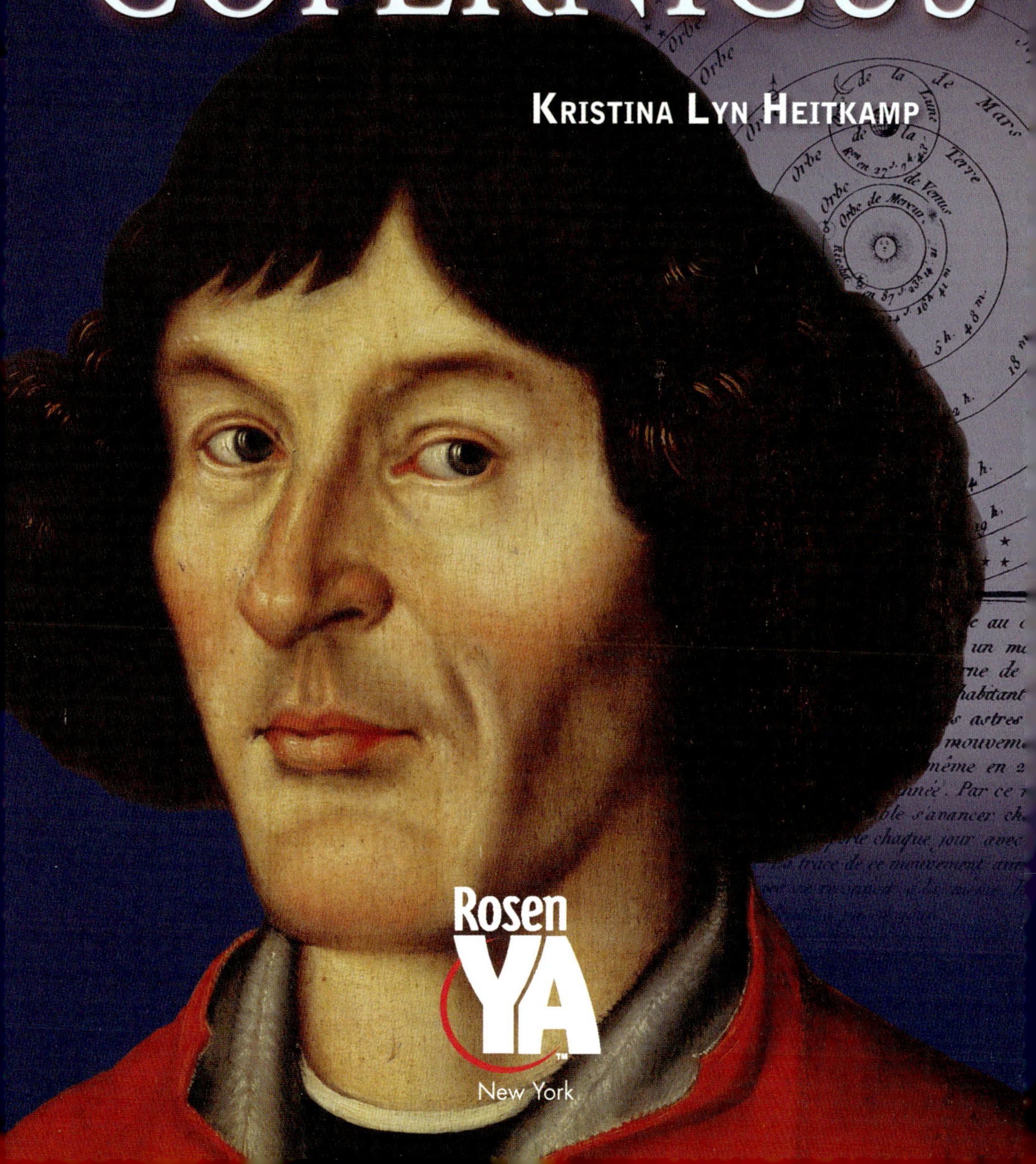

KRISTINA LYN HEITKAMP

Rosen YA™

New York

Published in 2018 by The Rosen Publishing Group, Inc.
29 East 21st Street, New York, NY 10010

First Edition

Library of Congress Cataloging-in-Publication Data

Names: Heitkamp, Kristina Lyn, author.
Title: Nicolaus Copernicus/Kristina Lyn Heitkamp.
Description: First edition. | New York: Rosen Publishing, 2018. | Series: Leaders of the scientific revolution | Audience: Grade 7–12. | Includes bibliographical references and index.
Identifiers: LCCN 2016055889 | ISBN 9781508174745 (library bound)
Subjects: LCSH: Copernicus, Nicolaus, 1473–1543—Juvenile literature. | Astronomers—Poland—Biography—Juvenile literature. | Astronomy—History—Juvenile literature.
Classification: LCC QB36.C8 H335 2018 | DDC 520.92 [B]—dc23
LC record available at https://lccn.loc.gov/2016055889

Manufactured in China

On the cover: Detail of the anonymous portrait of Copernicus in the town hall of Toruń, Poland.

CONTENTS

INTRODUCTION 4

CHAPTER ONE
PRECURSORS AND INFLUENCERS 8

CHAPTER TWO
HOME SWEET HOME 23

CHAPTER THREE
HIT THE BOOKS 36

CHAPTER FOUR
A MAN FOR ALL SEASONS 50

CHAPTER FIVE
BRAGGING RIGHTS 66

CHAPTER SIX
COPERNICAN REVOLUTION 81

TIMELINE 96
GLOSSARY 98
FOR MORE INFORMATION 101
FOR FURTHER READING 104
BIBLIOGRAPHY 106
INDEX 108

Introduction

When a supergiant dies, it goes out with a big bang. After burning for many years, the star expands, collapses, and then violently spews its insides out across the universe, spreading stardust and creating a supernova explosion. Whether it's at a supernova blowing its innards out or the glistening tail of a periodic comet, people have looked up above to the changing night sky and contemplated their place in the universe. By the fourth century BCE, the general consensus was that the earth was the center of the universe. This belief system remained unchallenged for almost two thousand years until a quiet, unassuming man wondered if his predecessors had gotten it wrong.

Known as the father of modern astronomy, Nicolaus Copernicus was a Polish astronomer who lived during the progressive golden period of the Renaissance. A scholarly man, he treated patients as a doctor, practiced church law as a canon, tried to reform currency, and even protected territory from the Teutonic Knights. In his free time, he studied the night sky. He spent more than thirty years diligently observing and recording the heavens. He analyzed the ideas of ancient astronomers and crunched geometric numbers.

The artist of this sixteenth-century portrait of Nicolaus Copernicus is unknown. A man of many talents, Copernicus was also an artist.

He was determined to find evidence that supported a heliocentric universe—a model where the sun, not the earth, resides at the center. Yet Copernicus barely whispered a word about his work.

In many ways, Copernicus was much like a supernova. Like a star, he quietly burned brightly for several years. He fused elements of discovery together, reaching degrees of calculation and expanding knowledge. His life's work, *De Revolutionibus Orbium Coelestium* (*On the Revolutions of the Heavenly Spheres*)—often known simply as *De Revolutionibus*—was published on his deathbed, yet the knowledge gleaned from his book remained a glowing beacon of modern science and profound insight for years to come. Its publication spurred a network of events and fundamentally changed humankind's understanding of the universe and beyond.

A catalyst for the Scientific Revolution, Copernicus's publication *De Revolutionibus* overturned ancient ideologies of the Middle Ages. It laid the foundation for other major players in the Scientific Revolution, such as Johannes Kepler and Galileo Galilei. The theories asserted in Copernicus's work furthered the modern understanding of scientific discovery and humankind's identity and relationship with the universe. The Scientific Revolution refers to a time in European history, roughly 1550 to 1700, when scientific, philosophical, and religious thoughts and beliefs were changing.

Some historians may argue about the exact timeline of the Scientific Revolution and who exactly qualifies as revolutionary contributors, but scholars agree that it all began with Copernicus. German scientist and poet Johann Wolfgang von Goethe concisely described the influence of Copernicus as follows:

> **Of all discoveries and opinions, none may have exerted a greater effect on the human spirit than the doctrine of Copernicus. The world had scarcely become known as round and complete in itself when it was asked to waive the tremendous privilege of being the center of the universe. Never, perhaps, was a greater demand made on mankind—for by this admission so many things vanished in mist and smoke! What became of our Eden, our world of innocence, piety and poetry; the testimony of the senses; the conviction of a poetic—religious faith? No wonder his contemporaries did not wish to let all this go and offered every possible resistance to a doctrine which in its converts authorized and demanded a freedom of view and greatness of thought so far unknown, indeed not even dreamed of.**

CHAPTER ONE

Precursors and Influencers

Although he was an active doctor and man of the church, Nicolaus Copernicus worked most of his astronomical life in seclusion. Tucked away in his house in a remote part of the world, Copernicus did not have other astronomers nearby to discuss and debate the theories of the universe. Although he was alone with his thoughts, he was in the company of other great thinkers of the past through their publications. The titles collected in Copernicus's library were a source of inspiration and yet a cause for frustration.

AT THE CENTER OF EVERYTHING

Much like Copernicus, the great ancient Greek philosopher and scientist Aristotle used observation and logic to arrive at his model of the universe. Early minds awed by the changing sky wished to make sense of it all and to bring a sense of comfort to observers. Intellectual minds of the fourth century BCE wanted to believe the universe was perfect and unchanging.

A student of the philosopher Plato, Aristotle studied philosophy and physics of the heavens. Plato believed the universe was comprised of perfect spherical shapes. Aristotle furthered Plato's belief and claimed Earth was the fixed center of the cosmos. From observations, Aristotle concluded that Earth was spherical (it is actually a lumpy, shifting spherical shape, not perfect at all). First he noticed that departing ships seemed to sink into the horizon. Ships got smaller and smaller as if they were sailing across a large ball. He also witnessed the round shape of Earth's shadow during a lunar eclipse. Aristotle put two and two together to claim that the planet was indeed round.

Aristotle thought it was just common sense that Earth was not in motion. He didn't feel it moving. When an apple fell from a tree, it dropped straight to the ground. If Earth were in motion, wouldn't the apple fly off? Imagine an apple falling from a window of a moving car. Instead of dropping, it first soars through the air and then later falls to the ground. Today we know this happens because of gravity, but Aristotle explained it as Earth's prized placement at the center of the universe and the work of the prime mover.

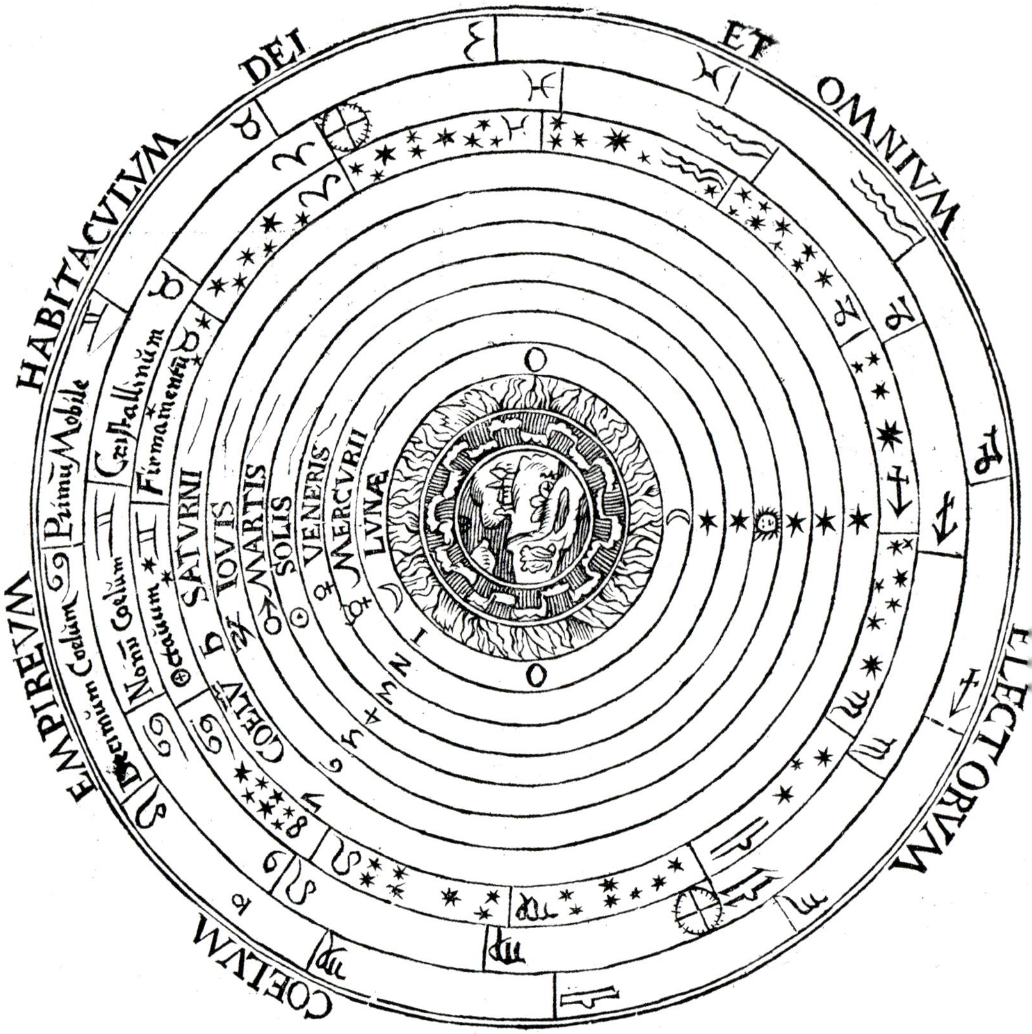

This diagram showing an Earth-centered universe with spheres of the planets was published in *Cosmographia,* written by the German geographer Petrus Apianus in 1524.

Aristotle said that all movement had a mover, just like an open door needs a hand, shoulder, or foot to move it. But for him, movement was more than just the act of pushing a door open. He believed it was a network of events. The prime mover caused movement, but it didn't initiate it. It was the unmoved mover of the universe. It was the be-all and end-all of all movements.

Christian thinkers came to identify Aristotle's prime mover with the God of Christian theology. Aristotle's model established the geocentric, or Earth-centered, universe. The prime mover, or God, proved to be a contrary component for Copernicus. His new model of the universe pushed the prime mover out. Yet he devoted his life to the Catholic Church. Copernicus's dedication to the church could have been a contributing reason why he waited until his deathbed to hand his Earth-moving manuscript over to the printers.

EARTH RULES

One of the most influential Greek astronomers and geographers, Claudius Ptolemy crafted a geocentric model of the universe that was eventually adopted by the church and remained part of popular belief for almost two thousand years, until Copernicus dared to challenge it.

Although Aristotle's model of the universe offered a comforting ideal, Ptolemy realized that the model needed a little fine-tuning to make the perfect cut. Some things were off and needed an explanation. Sometimes planets seemed to move three steps forward, then ten steps back, and finally continued forward again. The

IN A WORLD OF HIS OWN

The Greek mathematician and astronomer Aristarchus of Samos lived during the third century BCE in Alexandria, Egypt. Using observation, logic, and geometry, he was the first to propose a sun-centered, or heliocentric, universe. Aristarchus determined through observation that the sun was much bigger and farther away than the moon. He claimed the sun was the fixed center of the universe, with Earth and all the other planets revolving around it. Yet it would take another few thousand years, and the observations and data collected by Copernicus, for anyone else to consider a heliocentric model.

Aristarchus also attempted to measure the sizes of the sun, the moon, and Earth, as well as the distances between all three. Even though his measurements were not very accurate, he still demonstrated an understanding of sizes and relative distances. However, his ideas were not accepted by the Greeks and garnered little attention. His heliocentric theory never gained momentum and easily slipped away into a void. Unfortunately, his work that discussed the sun-centered universe model was lost. His ideas have been pieced together from later work and references.

Aristarchus's work was an inspiration for Copernicus. In fact, in a draft of his famous work *De Revolutionibus*, Copernicus cites Aristarchus and his authority in bumping Earth from its valued central position. But Copernicus later crossed out the reference. It is often debated which great mind was the true originator of the breakthrough. Although the heliocentric universe is most often attributed to Copernicus, Aristarchus played a supporting role.

apparent backward track of planets against the backdrop of stars caused confusion. Scientists now have a name for the apparent shuffle—retrograde motion. This phenomenon is actually an illusion. The motion of Earth causes the appearance of movement. For example, every two years or so the illusion of Mars's retrograde motion is caused by the way Earth and Mars orbit the sun. Like two cars on a racetrack, Earth moves on the inside lane orbiting faster than Mars on an outside lane. When Earth laps Mars, it appears as if the red planet is moving backward.

Ptolemy explained retrograde motion by attaching each planet to two spheres. The main larger sphere was called the deferent. Planets orbited around the earth on the deferent. The second, smaller sphere was called

This portrait of Claudius Ptolemy is by Pedro Berruguete and Juste De Fand. The astronomer was also a great geographer. Christopher Columbus and Magellan used Ptolemy's maps to guide voyages.

an epicycle. Planets also rotated on their own personal epicycle. When combined, the planetary motion caused by the deferent and epicycle created the one step forward and two step back shuffle. The Ptolemaic system was unnecessarily complicated and needed tinkering. More epicycles were later added to convolute the model even further. Although it was incredibly complex, Ptolemy's system worked fairly well. His predictions of celestial movements were mostly accurate. Plus, they kept Earth in its esteemed location, center stage in the universe.

Ptolemy documented his life work in an all-encompassing work titled *Mathematike Syntaxis* (*The Mathematical Arrangement)*; often known as the *Almagest.*) The *Almagest* was divided into thirteen different books covering an encyclopedic amount of astronomical concepts about the universe. The title remained the basis for astronomical truth for over a thousand years. It was used as a guide for Islamic and European astronomers,and was translated into Arabic and Latin. The comprehensive textbook of ancient astronomy contained a star catalog and an explanation of all the spheres of the planets. It charted and predicted the positions of heavenly bodies, and also included Ptolemy's explanation of the retrograde motion.

Although Copernicus studied and learned from the *Almagest*, the complexity of the Ptolemaic model bothered him. If the universe was a perfect creation, why consideratioñe patuit:erit ⁊ locus augis facilime cognitus. Ptolemeus eni distantiam tertie habitudinis ab auge numerauit.51.gradus:⁊.14.minuta. Erat aũt locus huius tertie habitudinis verus in.14.gra.⁊.14.minu.capri/corni.quare cõtra signorum consequentiam a.14.mi.14.gra.capricorni si nu merauerimus.51.gradus ⁊.14.minuta:ad finem.23.gradus.46.minu.scor/pionis perueniemus:In quo etiam Ptolemeus augi locum in principio re/gni Antonij deputauit.

Propositio xv.

IN qua vo parte zodiaci saturni locus medius sit in aliqua trium habitudinũ:quantũq3 ab auge epi/cycli media distet inuestigare.

¶Locus augis iam notus est ex precedenti. Media vo vniuscuiusq3 trium habitudinũ ab auge distantia superius inuenta est:quare medius locus erit notus. Q3 si super puncto.g.tertie habitudinis epicyclum.h.t.k.descripserimus:erit arcus.h.t.k.distantie planete ab auge epicycli media in tertia habitudine nõ ignotus. Est eni angulus.g.z.l.cogni tus ex.12.huius. Sed ⁊ angulus.g.e.l.vere distãtie tertie habitudinis ab au ge per.13.notus.quare residuus intrinsecus.e.g.z.cognitus:⁊ arcus.t.k.nu/meratus. Quem si a semicirculo.h.t.dempseris : relinquetur arcus.h.k.qui querebatur notus.

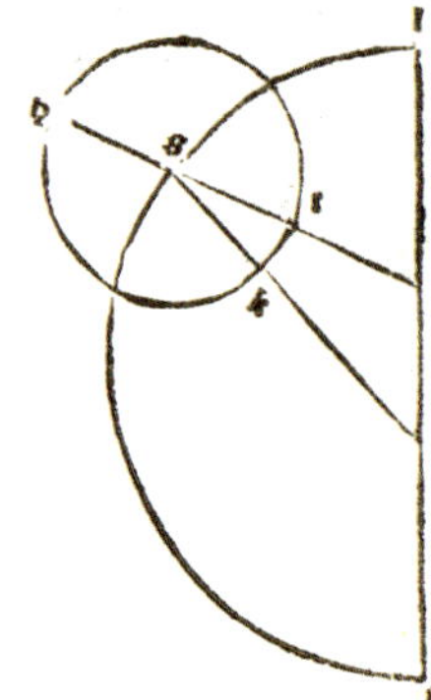

Propositio xvj.

ECentrici ⁊ epicycli duab⁹ semidiametris ligã pro/portionibus elaborare.

¶Certissima quadam ad hoc propositum opus est considera tione. Ptolemeus noster in anno secundo Antonij : sexto die mensis Mesir : sexti sc3 transacto:ante medietatem noctis.4. horis equalibus Saturni locũ instrumẽto suo ad Aldebaran rectificato ⁊ ad lunam relatione:deprehendit in.9.g̃.⁊.4.m̃.aquarij : dũ sc3 medium celi instrumẽto indice esset in Alexandria vltimus gradus arietis. et sol cursu suo medio in.28.partibus ⁊.41.minutis sagittarij.Estimauit aũt inter cornu septentrionale ⁊ saturnum tunc ƀm visum quidem cadere.30.m̃. ad successionem signorum.Sed locus visus lune tunc ƀm numeratioñe Pto lemei fuit in.8.gradu ⁊.34.minu.aquarij.vnde certus fuit locus saturni. Et quia tempus:quod intercedit huic ꝯsiderationi ⁊ habitudini tertie superius memorate notum erat : notus fuit medius motus lõgitudinis saturni in hoc tempore.Qui tametsi nondum rectificatus habeatur:tamen non poterit sen sibilem in hoc opere errorem ingerere. Erat etiam medius locus saturni in hac habitudine tertia notus:quare ⁊ in hac cõsideratione motus medius sa turni non ignorabitur. Simili pacto distantia lune ab auge epicycli media in hac consideratione innotuit. ¶Post hec itaq3 recitata pingamus circu/lum eccentricum epicycli delatorem.a.b.g.super centro.d. In cuius diame/tro.a.g.punctus.a.sit aux.g.oppositum augis.z.centrum equantis.⁊.e.cen/trum mundi.Sitq3 in eius circũferentia punctus.b.centrum epicycli.h.t.k. et locus planete in eodem punctus.k.productis lineis.e.b.t.et.d.b.et.z.b.h. erit.h.aux media epicycli.et.t.aux vera.Itẽq3 due linee.e.k.et.b.k.producã tur:dueq3 perpendiculares.d.m.et.e.l.super lineam.b.l.aliaq3 perpendicu/

n

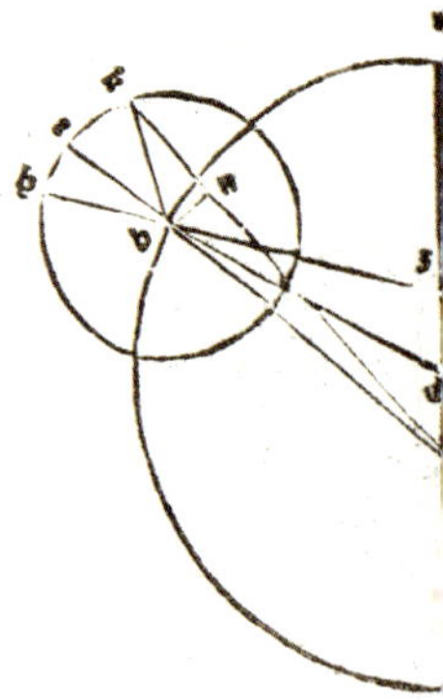

These illustrations, from an early edition of Ptolemy's Almagest, on this page show the epicycles that the author used to explain Saturn's apparent retrograde motion.

was it so complicated? Copernicus set out to solve the mystery of the universe and make it picture perfect.

KEEP IT SIMPLE

The Ptolemaic model of the universe was needlessly complicated, stretching numbers and circles to match movement in the sky. Most people accepted the geocentric model, but a few intellectuals, including Copernicus, found trouble with it and pursued a simpler system.

Attributed to fourteenth-century logician and Franciscan friar William of Ockham, Occam's (or Ockham's) razor is the principle that "entities should not be multiplied unnecessarily." Plainly put, the simplest explanation is often the best one. For example, you're out on a walk and notice a tree has been split right down the center. The edges of the cut are crispy and charred. Either an alien spaceship blasted the tree with its laser beam or it was struck by lightning during a recent thunderstorm. Occam's razor would point to the uncluttered answer, which doesn't require more probing or questions. Therefore, the tree was struck by lightning. The fewer assumptions made, the closer one is to a more elegant theory that explains the perfect nature of the universe.

BLAZING THE TRAIL

During the fifteenth century, astronomers were faced with several inaccuracies, including astronomical tables that failed to correctly predict events. The yearly calendar was no longer accurate. The equinox had fallen outside the date predicted, and because religious holidays were determined with reference to the equinox, the calendar was a complete mess.

The reformation of European astronomy began with a student and his teacher, about fifty years before Copernicus was born. Johann Müller von Königsberg, better known as Regiomontanus, was a student of Georg von Peuerbach's at the University of Vienna, in Austria. Peuerbach authored astronomical yearbooks that projected the movement of the sun, moon, and planets. He also served as a court astrologer to the king of Hungary. His student and later colleague Regiomontanus was an Austrian observational astronomer and gifted mathematician. Additionally, he could read and speak Greek. After graduating from college at the age of fifteen, Regiomontanus worked alongside Peuerbach on several astronomical projects. Both men were interested in fixing astronomical inaccuracies.

Peuerbach's best-known work, titled *Theoricae Novae Planetarum* (*New Theories of the Planets*), suggested that the sun governed the planets' movements. The work,

Regiomontanus was an ambitious and brilliant prodigy, entering the University of Leipzig at the young age of eleven years old.

which was very influential in planetary theory, eventually made it into the hands of Copernicus.

Peuerbach was also tasked to write a new Latin translation of Ptolemy's *Almagest.* Unfortunately, a year into his work he fell ill. He asked his partner, Regiomontanus, to finish his work. Peuerbach died before the work was completed, when he was just thirty-eight years old. Regiomontanus finished the *Epytoma Joannis de Monte Regio in Almagestum Ptolomei* (Johann Regiomontanus's Epitome of the *Almagest* of Ptolemy), often called simply the *Epitome.* This included his own commentary and new observations. He also further developed the trigonometric studies that Peuerbach had started. Trigonometry was a very important tool and was used to measure the positions of heavenly bodies. Regiomontanus completed several more works, one of which was among the first books that Copernicus purchased for his personal library titled *Tabulae Directionum* (*Tables of Directions*). The tables assisted in determining the position of the celestial bodies based on the rotation of the night sky.

Regiomontanus was suspicious of the Ptolemaic system of the universe, and he knew it needed updating. He set out to revamp the astronomical system. First on his to-do list was to publish important mathematic and astronomical works. This was quite a daunting task, but not as ambitious as his second goal—to start from ground zero and make new observations of the universe. Regiomontanus moved to Nuremberg, Germany, so he could have access to helpful astronomical instruments and the great minds of many learned people in the city. He set up a printing press in his new house and, with the help of a benefactor, built an astronomical observatory above the city. He created a list of books with at least twenty classics that he planned to translate into Latin and publish. Also on the list were twenty-one projects that he intended to author.

Regiomontanus was a crusader for getting mathematic and astronomy classics into the hands of many. However, like Peuerbach, he also died young—at the age of forty—before his mission was complete.

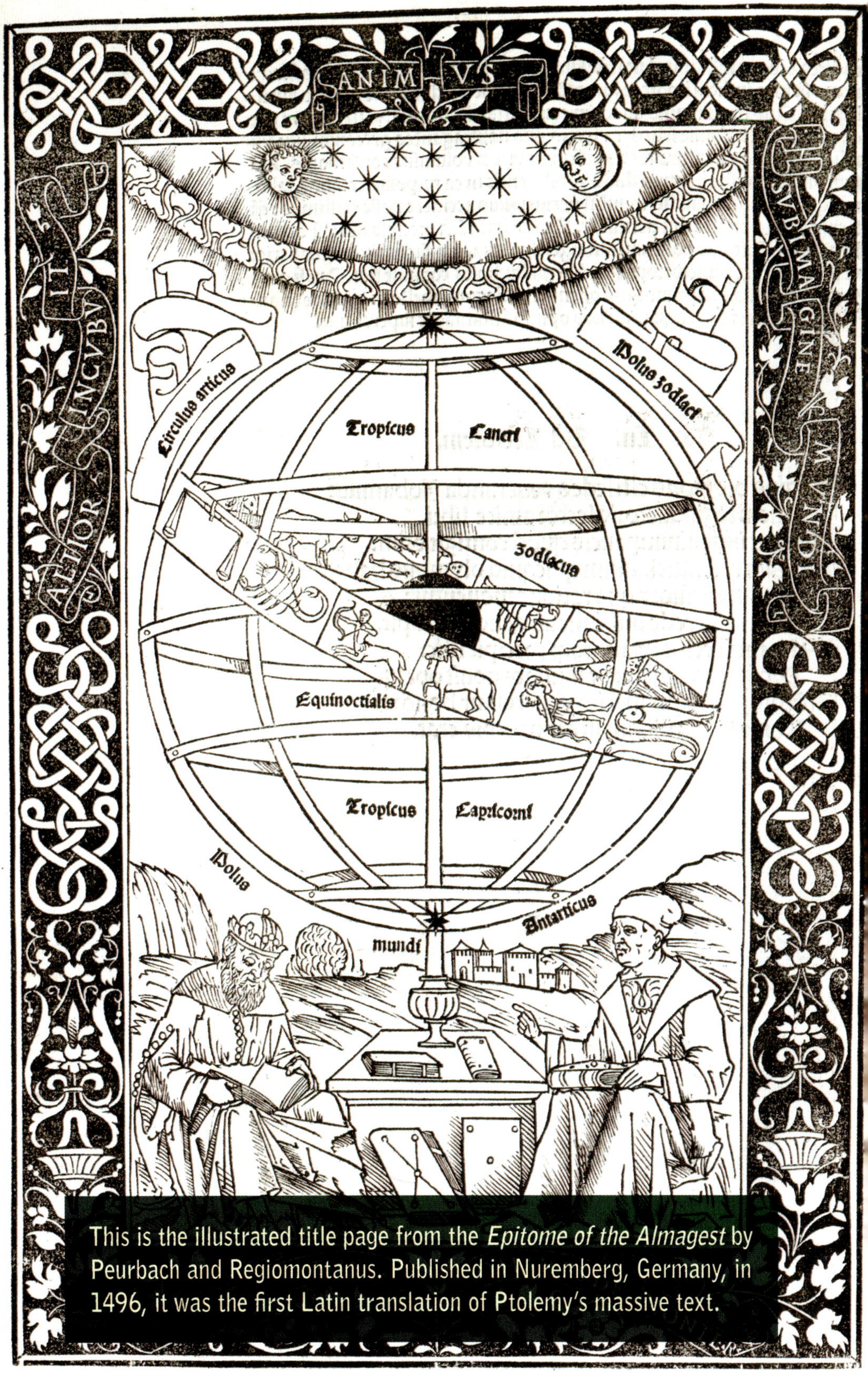

This is the illustrated title page from the *Epitome of the Almagest* by Peurbach and Regiomontanus. Published in Nuremberg, Germany, in 1496, it was the first Latin translation of Ptolemy's massive text.

Whether it was a two-thousand-year-old book densely packed with ideas or a newer release with a hint of innovation, the books Copernicus read encouraged him to further develop his understanding of the complex universe. Without the foundation set by trailblazers, Copernicus may not have set forth and formulated his model of the universe.

CHAPTER TWO

HOME SWEET HOME

Copernicus's legacy can be seen near and far. One of the largest lunar craters bears his name. Copernicum is a radioactive element found on the periodic table. *Copernica*, or the tree of life, is a genus of palm trees with large fanned leaves that is native to Cuba and South America. But before his widespread fame, Nicolaus Copernicus was an ordinary kid growing up in an extraordinary time.

FLESH AND BLOOD

Born on February 19, 1473, Mikolaj Kopernik (best known by his Latinized name Nicolaus Copernicus) came into the world on a cold winter day in Toruń, Poland. He was the baby of the family with three older

The Copernicus family owned several houses in Toruń, Poland. The home depicted in this lithograph is thought to be where Nicolaus was born.

siblings. He had one brother who was about seven years older named Andreas, and two sisters, Catherine and Barbara. His father, also named Nicolaus, was a successful copper merchant. His mother, Barbara Watzenrode, came from one of the wealthiest families in Toruń.

The Copernicus family lived quite well, with several servants in their luxurious three-story home near the center of the bustling trade town. They owned a vineyard and other properties outside of the city. Toruń was a trading hub with a population of about twenty thousand people. Massive regional markets were held each week in the town square. Nicolaus may have tagged along with his big brother to watch the emporium of trade at the regional market, spying on foreign merchants and their goods. The Copernicus brothers may have raced down the cobblestone streets to a bridge their father had funded to reach the waters of the Vistula River, which flows into the Baltic Sea. Nicolaus may have splashed in the river while his brother hunted for game. Or perhaps the brothers fought pretend battles with stick-swords in the ruins of a nearby castle that had belonged to the Teutonic Knights. Toruń was likely an exciting place to grow up.

HEARTH AND HOME

The city of Toruń boasts a complex history with a rich cultural heritage. It has been ruled by both the Prussians and the Polish crown. The Swedes tore through the area in a siege during the Second Northern War, a hundred years after Copernicus's time, and Napoleon and his forces spent a brief stint there as well. Even Hitler occupied Toruń for a time. It has been home to a variety of people from varying nations and of varying religions. This area has been fought over many times throughout history.

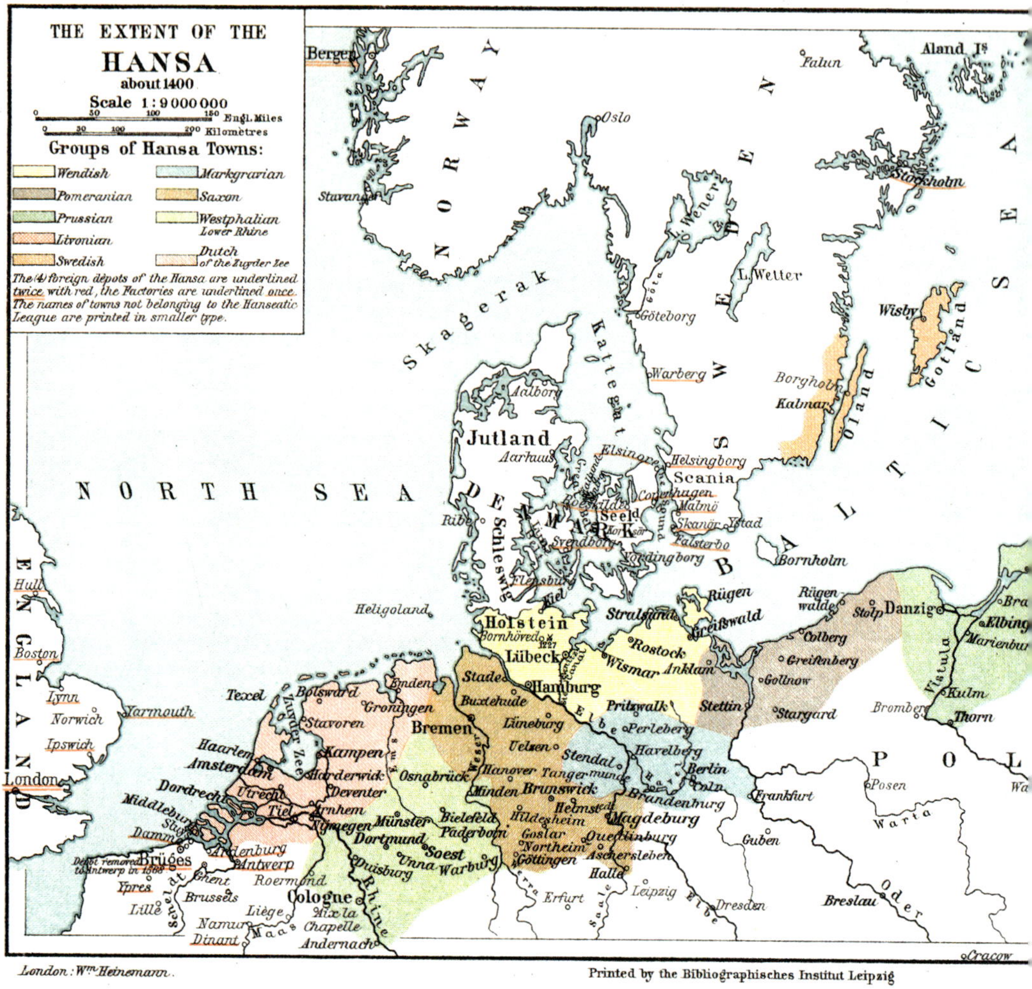

During the fourteenth century, Toruń was part of the Hanseatic League, a trade alliance established along the coast of Northern Europe to monopolize the trading route. This map uses the town's German name, Thorn.

First established in 1231 by the Teutonic Knights, Toruń remained under Teutonic rule for more than two centuries. Formed during Holy Roman emperor

New York: Dodd, Mead & C°

Henry VI's Holy Crusade, the Teutonic Knights were a religious army tasked with colonizing and converting pagans, or non-Christians, across European lands. When the Crusades ended, the knights were invited to the Baltic region to Christianize the natives. Any land the knights conquered, they were told to keep. Members of the order eagerly devoured the opportunity. They settled Toruń, building permanent homes and an impressive castle. They established their own kingdom, the Teutonic Order State of Prussia. They spread out, building up over seventy towns. Some of the buildings still stand today, including parts of the castle in Toruń.

Although the Teutonic Knights dominated substantial territory, the Kingdom of Poland and the citizens of Prussia grew weary of the knights' oppressive rule and hostility. The knights had blocked off access to the Baltic Sea and slaughtered and enslaved many Prussians. A rebellion broke out in Toruń in 1454, and a thirteen-year war followed. Copernicus's father was in Toruń doing business at this time, and he eventually met and married Barbara. The knights were finally defeated, and a peace treaty was signed in 1466. The Teutonic Order State of Prussia was renamed Royal Prussia and fell under the rule of the king of Poland, although he gave the area a lot of freedom. The Teutonic Knights still occupied surrounding lands and continued to pester Royal Prussia over the years. Copernicus would come face-to-face with the Teutonic Knights later in his life.

NAME AND NATIONALITY

While all agree that Nicolaus Copernicus is the father of modern astronomy, a tug of war has erupted over who lays claim to his legacy. Germans celebrate the German scientist Nikolaus Koppernik, while the Poles honor their great Polish astronomer Mikolaj Kopernik. The truth is that Copernicus and his contemporaries were indifferent to nationality. Toruń was home to a diverse group of people over a long period of time. When Copernicus was born, Toruń was under rule of the Polish king, so technically he was born a citizen of Poland. He spoke German, but there is ample evidence that he also knew the Polish language. All his astronomical work was written in Latin, as was most scholarly work at that time. Poland may argue that Copernicus was Polish based on how he defended Royal Prussia (under Polish rule) against the Teutonic Knights.

In 1410, the Battle of Tanneberg in northeastern Poland marked the beginning of the end of Teutonic rule. The gruesome ten-hour battle claimed the lives of 205 Teutonic Knights.

But Germany may argue that although he lived in Royal Prussia, he maintained cultural ties with their country because German was his mother tongue. Plus, his mother and grandmother were immigrants from Germany.

Some historians see the debate as insignificant because nationalism is a modern idea. It wasn't until the nineteenth century that nationalism planted its roots in the hearts of patriots in Europe. Nationalism celebrates a common origin, ethnicity, and cultural ties. But even the ideology of national identity is debated. What defines a person as Polish, German, or American? Some philosophers say nationalism is dependent on two things. The first is being proud of your nation and caring about national identity. Second is taking action to preserve national identity. But others wonder if nationalism is a voluntary or involuntary concept. Is national identity determined by where one is born or by which country flag a person waves proud and high in his or her heart?

CURRENT STATE OF AFFAIRS

Nicolaus Copernicus was born on the tail end of a period in European history called the Renaissance, which lasted from roughly 1375 to 1575. It was an exciting time of intellectual discovery. Everything was changing. There were new developments in art, science, and philosophy.

Advancements in technology were changing education and communication.

Copernicus grew up in an environment that kindled new ideas and fostered exploration of those ideas. His young mind was likely stimulated in many ways. But the development that most influenced Copernicus was the invention of the printing press.

In 1436, a German goldsmith named Johannes Gutenberg began tinkering with a machine that could produce pages of text in little time. Previously, printers carved text onto a block of wood, smeared ink on the surface, and laid a sheet of paper on top. The process was time consuming and costly. Gutenberg's printing press employed reusable and movable individual letter type that could be arranged into words. He also created a special water-based ink that transferred more effectively to the paper. Once the letters were arranged and coated with ink, a screw press (similar to a modern-day drill press) lowered the text onto a sheet of paper and pressed. With the new process, whole pages of texts were quickly printed.

By 1454, Gutenberg put his press to commercial use and produced several works for the church. The first printed book was the Bible. Gutenberg printed about two hundred copies, and each came with a hefty price tag. Within a few years, printing presses had sprung up all over Europe, printing titles about science, religion, medicine, and history.

Printing with wood blocks had been done before, but Johannes Gutenberg was the first to use a huge press and moveable type to print text on large sheets of paper.

The printing revolution spread ideas and knowledge across Europe. Copernicus had access to the mass production of information. He could read translations of ancient texts or peruse the charts and diagrams of

astronomical works. Later, it would give him the opportunity to share his ideas with the world.

WINDS OF CHANGE

When Copernicus was ten years old, his father died. Unfortunately, near the end of his life, the once-successful copper merchant had fallen into financial trouble. But luckily for the Copernicus brothers, their mother's brother, Lucas Watzenrode, was well established, wealthy, and, at that time, childless. He agreed to become the boys' benefactor.

Uncle Lucas was a church canon of the Frombork chapter and later became the elected bishop of Warmia, a senior position of great respect. He resolved to take the boys under his wing and secure them a good future. First he wanted the boys to get a good education.

MAKE AN APPEARANCE

Copernicus's mug has been on a series of stamps and Polish currency. However, there are very few portraits of him. What did he look like? One painted portrait hangs in the town hall of Toruń. Another portrait, on the astronomical clock of Strasbourg Cathedral, in France, claims to be a copy of an original. The artist, Tobias Stimmer, was said to have used Copernicus's own self-portrait as a guide or study for his painting. But modern science had given us a glimpse into the face of the past.

After Copernicus died in 1543, his body was laid to rest below the floor of Frombork Cathedral. His grave was unmarked, and the exact location was forgotten. In the summers of 2004 and 2005, archaeologists tackled the mystery of the missing bones. They excavated the sections neighboring the altar where they thought Copernicus was buried. In the very lowest level of dirt, they found a scattering of old bones that belonged to a sixty- to seventy-year-old man. Copernicus was seventy years old when he died. Archaeologists pulled out a cranium but did not find a mandible.

Back at the forensics lab, experts compared DNA found in a well-preserved cranial tooth in the skull to hairs found in a book from Copernicus's personal library. It was a match. Next researchers used the same method that police employ to flesh out the features of a decomposed murder victim to build a forensic reconstruction of Copernicus's face. They compared the computer-generated image to portraits. They discovered matching evidence of a nose that had been broken a few times, as well as a forehead scar.

Copernicus's remains were placed in a wooden coffin and laid in state for several weeks. This is a tradition where the deceased is available for public viewing. Afterward, his coffin toured regions and towns linked to his life. Then his remains were blessed with holy water by Poland's notable clerics and lowered back into the ground where he had been found under the cathedral floor. A black granite tombstone decorated with a model of the solar system now marks his grave.

In 1491, Nicolaus and Andreas left their hometown of Toruń, perhaps for the very first time, and set off for university.

CHAPTER THREE

Hit the Books

Uncle Lucas was a wealthy and powerful man. He wanted to make sure his nephews had the same experiences that many of the men in their family had—to travel the world and receive the best education. Nicolaus was almost nineteen when he started his venture into academia. He would travel, learn, debate, and discuss for the next ten or so years.

STARS IN HIS EYES

Nicolaus and his brother, Andreas, started their adventure in the celebrated capital of the Kingdom of Poland, Kraków. In the autumn of 1491, both boys enrolled at their uncle's alma mater, the University of Kraków. The university was among the most prestigious institutions

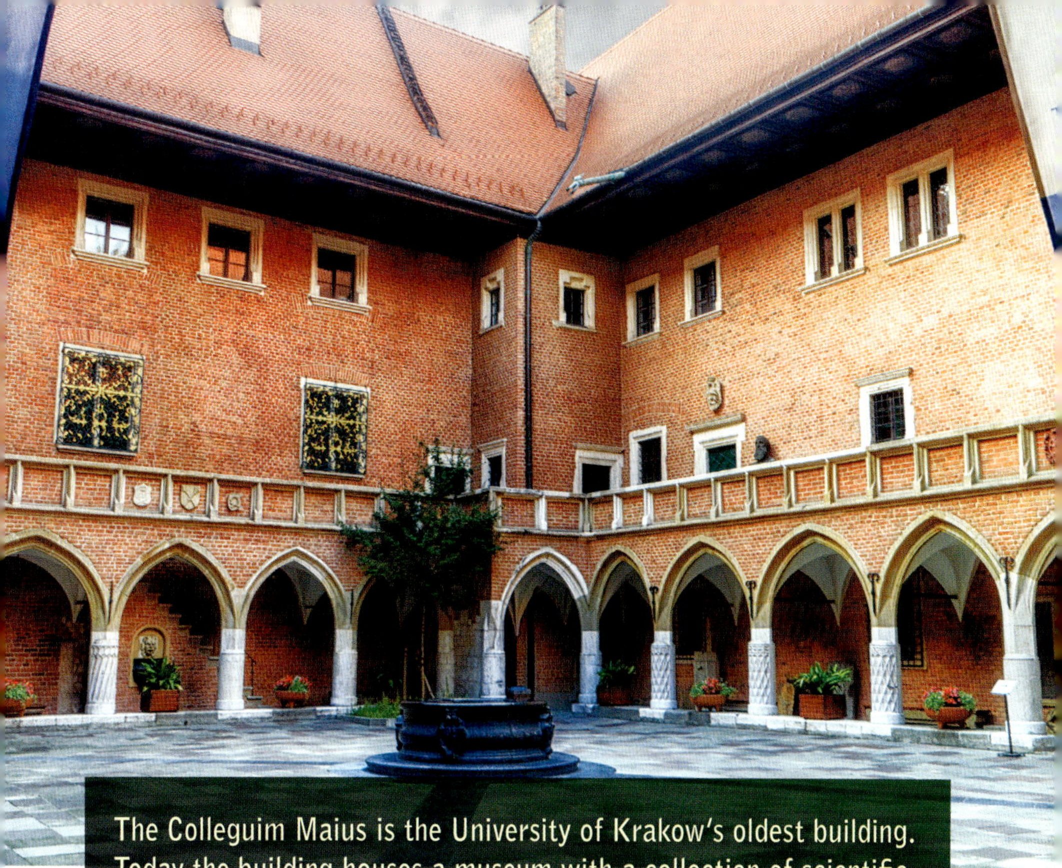

The Colleguim Maius is the University of Krakow's oldest building. Today the building houses a museum with a collection of scientific instruments, including tools Copernicus may have used.

in Europe. It was known for its high level of instruction in the liberal arts, mathematics, and astronomy. The school attracted students from all over the country and outside Poland, including Hungary, Scandinavia, and Italy. The city of Kraków was also a "happening" place, enticing scholars, entertainers, and visitors from all over the world.

The Copernicus brothers did not stay in student housing with their classmates, instead living with their uncle's friend Piotr Wapowski and his son Bernard. Nicolaus and Bernard became good friends and stayed in touch over the years. Bernard eventually became a leading cartographer, or maker of maps.

Copernicus took courses from the standard curriculum: philosophy, law, Latin, and theology. The university boasted a highly distinguished astronomy and astrology department, offering several courses in mathematics and sciences. The department provided Copernicus an excellent comprehensive education in astronomic sciences. He also took courses in meteorology, surveying, and geography. He studied the classics, such as Aristotle and Ptolemy, but he also studied the works of contemporary astronomers. When Professor Albert Brudzewski lectured on the work of Peuerbach and Regiomontanus, he may have expressed his skepticism of the geocentric model of the universe. In the same building where Copernicus learned about Peuerbach's theory of the planets, there was an astronomical observatory on the rooftop, from which he may have witnessed his first lunar eclipse.

The university was also well stocked with astronomical instruments. Marcin Bylica, a Polish astronomer who had collaborated with Regiomontanus on a few projects, had attended the university. He later bequeathed his astronomical instruments to the school. Included in his gift was an enormous armillary sphere, which is a movable model of the celestial globe with rings and hoops representing the different celestial spheres. The

An armillary sphere helped Copernicus visualize Ptolemy's geocentric model of the universe. The spherical rings that turned around Earth at the center indicated the celestial spheres.

WRITTEN IN THE STARS

Almost every US newspaper features a daily horoscope offering advice on life decisions, what to expect in the coming month, and even warnings about possible conflicts that may arise. Horoscopes are supposedly a prediction of future events based on the positions of stars and planets at the time of a person's birth. Modern-day horoscopes are often read for entertainment, but not taken as truth or science. However, during the fifteenth and sixteenth centuries, astrology was considered a science. It was widely believed that the night sky influenced the lives and events of people on Earth.

Astrology was regarded as the practical application of theoretical astronomy. To be an astronomer meant one was also an astrologer. In fact, many notable astronomers made a living as astrologers, making predictions for kings and nobility by day and theorizing and contemplating astronomical ideas by night.

The need for accurate data and tables to make astrological predictions helped propel the science of astronomy. Copernicus took classes in astrology and studied the compiled lists of data, such as Regiomontanus's *Epitome*, that were used by astrologers. However, Copernicus did not make a living as an astrologer.

In 1524, several astrologers claimed that the end of the world was just around the corner. Astrologers interpreted the conjunction of Jupiter, Saturn, and Mars within the zodiac sign of Pisces to mean that an epic flood was about to envelope Earth. News of the fateful prophecy spread quickly. Few offered astrological evidence confirming the prophecy, while most called it a crazy delusion. Some people shrugged their shoulders, while others moved their families and built arks on mountaintops. However, the fateful day came and went without a flood. Historians suggest that the false prediction was the hook that pulled astrology out of the scientific sphere.

gift also included two flat Arabic metal astrolabes, used to calculate the position and latitude of celestial bodies, and a torquetum, used to determine ecliptic coordinates. Copernicus probably handled these instruments, using them as models for building his own.

During his time at the University of Kraków, Copernicus may have begun to question the geocentric model and wanted to further explore astronomy. Instead of sitting for exams at Kraków, he decided to continue his education.

BUILDING HIS CASE

After a brief stint back home with Uncle Lucas, Copernicus left Poland in 1496 and headed south to Bologna, Italy, to study law. The University of Bologna was one of the oldest and most respected universities in Europe. Uncle Lucas had also attended the university. Nicolaus enrolled in the School of Law to study canon law—a body of laws created by the church to govern the clergy

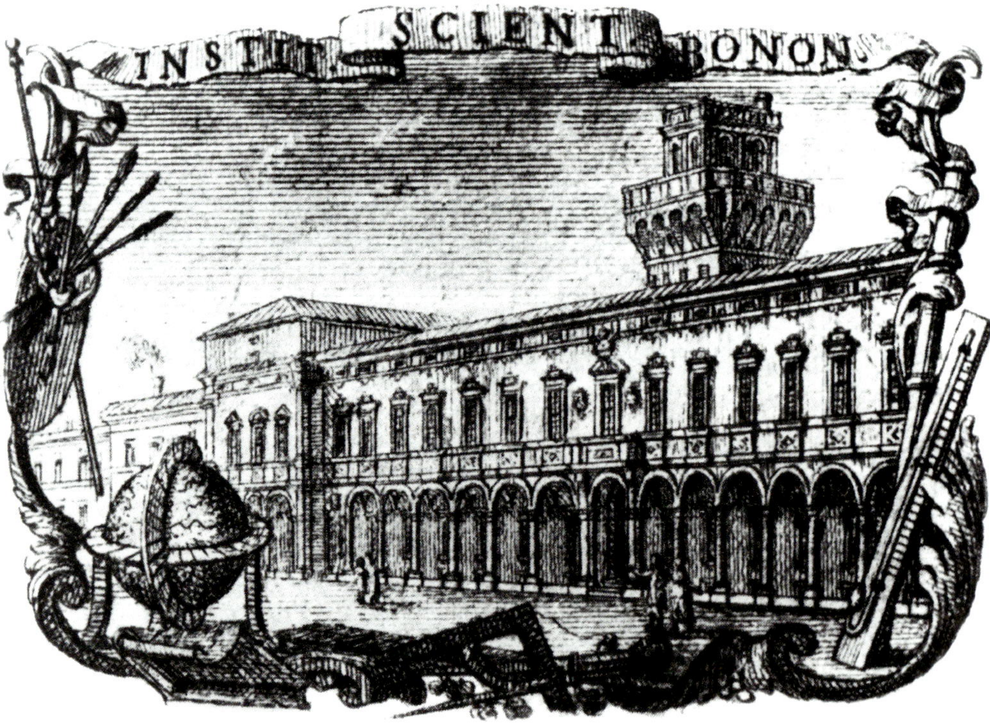

In 1088, the University of Bologna was established by a group of students who wanted to learn. The institution evolved to include instruction in law, medicine, philosophy, and theology.

and its members. Copernicus needed to learn the ins and outs of canon law in preparation for the position of canon at Frombork that his Uncle Lucas had arranged for him. A canon is an appointed church official who carries out the business of the church.

Although he had his nose stuck in law books, Copernicus still kept an eye toward the heavens. While at the university, he befriended a famous astronomy professor named Domenico Maria Novara, who had taught at the university for more than twenty years. Novara was tasked with producing an astrological almanac each year that included prophecies based on phases of the moon and the positions of the planets. Copernicus assisted him with his astronomical observations and helped out when needed. Novara quickly became an important mentor to him.

Copernicus made his first recorded observations while assisting Novara. On March 9, 1497, they observed a lunar occultation of the bright star Aldebaran. An occultation is when one celestial body passes in front of another, basically hiding it from view. The moon had eclipsed the star. Copernicus later referred to this observation in *De Revolutionibus* to support his theory of the motion of the moon. He also accompanied Novara to Rome for the Jubilee of 1500. A Jubilee, or holy year, is a yearlong Roman Catholic celebration of forgiveness of sins and reconciliation between adversaries. Copernicus proceeded to make more observations, including a lunar eclipse. He gave public lectures on mathematics, but the exact details of his talks are unknown.

After his education in Kraków and his time in Rome, Copernicus was expected to return to Poland to hold the canon position that Uncle Lucas had secured for him. He did return, but not to stay. Copernicus asked for a special leave of absence. He wasn't yet done with his studies.

JUST WHAT THE DOCTOR ORDERED

Copernicus's next education stop was the University of Padua, in Italy, to study medicine. The cathedral chapter in Frombork didn't have a doctor in their community, so Copernicus's medical studies would prepare him for an important part of the role that awaited him.

The University of Padua was one the best medical institutions in Europe. Medical education included not only the study of the human body, but also the study of the heavens. Because the celestial bodies were considered to have a major impact on people's lives, medical astronomy was studied to better understand how the stars affected human health. Diagnosis clues were found in horoscopes and the humors, while treatment would vary in accordance with planetary influence. Knowing how to interpret the stars and determine a patient's horoscope could be a matter of life or death.

For example, the then-common practice of bloodletting (drawing blood from a patient to prevent or cure an ailment) was thought to be risky if it was performed during the wrong part of an astrological cycle. The procedure was not done without consulting the moon's position and phase. Taking blood from a certain part of the body under a certain phase of the moon was said to result in excessive bleeding. Doctors consulted a diagram of the body, along with the patience's zodiac sign and astrological charts and calendars, before they would prick the skin for a drop of blood.

The university had top-notch professors who instructed students in both theoretical and practical medical studies. Students studied the healing properties of plants and herbs. Copernicus also learned about ancient authorities in medicine such as the father of Greek medicine, Hippocrates, and the father of medical research, Galen. Hippocrates employed the humoral theory, also called humorism. It was a model of how the body worked. Four humors represented different bodily elements: blood was air, phlegm was water, yellow bile was fire, and black bile was earth. The humors determined the health of the body and mind. Even a person's temperament was dependent on which humor was most dominant. Having a good balance of the four humors

The four humors were used to diagnose a patient's temperament. An excess of black bile could cause depression (bottom right). Too much yellow bile could make the patient irritable (bottom left).

meant you were in tip-top shape, both physically and mentally. But a humor imbalance could result in disease and dysfunction. The seasons and locations of planets also influenced these elements. A fuller moon resulted in an increased vulnerability to madness. Mars made people fickle, while Saturn increased sadness. Humoral theory was accepted in medical science and practice until the 1800s.

Copernicus studied human anatomy in an anatomic theater, where public dissections were performed. Human cadavers were sliced and diced publicly for medical students to glean information. The University of Padua was the first school to build a permanent theater to accommodate viewers at popular educational public dissections. Bodies were gathered from local hangings or donated by families who were offered a free funeral for their deceased loved one.

Copernicus likely accompanied his professors to visit the sick, shadowing the doctor and taking note of the physician's medical demeanor and advice. He also purchased medical textbooks, including *Practica Medicinae* (The Practice of Medicine) by Michele Savonarola. The comprehensive text included sections on proper decorum for physicians, pharmaceuticals and daily regimens, and a variety of diseases of the entire body. Copernicus likely later referenced this text while he was the resident physician at Frombork.

A diorama of the first permanent anatomy theater at the University of Padua. Professor of Anatomy and Surgery Girolamo Fabrici had the theater built in 1594.

During his time in Padua, Copernicus likely rubbed shoulders with the cultured city's active artist community. While interacting with artists in the area, he also learned how to sling paint onto a canvas. Of the few portraits of Copernicus from near the time he lived, one is thought to have been based on a self-portrait.

CAP AND GOWN

Copernicus studied at the University of Padua for two years, not completing the full program, which included two years of reading and discussion of the classics, followed by a third year of practical medicine and surgery. Copernicus never obtained his doctoral degree in medicine. He left Padua and headed to the University of Ferrara, also in Italy. Some scholars think that Copernicus was running out of money and time, so he jumped over to Ferrara for the cheaper tuition. He sat for his exams and received his doctorate in canon law. After more than ten years away, he returned to Poland in 1503. He was to begin his life as a canon and commence writing one of the most important texts of the Scientific Revolution.

CHAPTER FOUR

A Man for All Seasons

Armed with a doctorate in canon law, a personal library of astronomy books, and a headful of cosmic philosophies, Nicolaus Copernicus returned to his homeland of Poland. He was thirty years old, and his brain was likely brimming with astronomical ideas and inspirations. He'd been to Kraków, Bologna, Rome, Padua, and Ferrara. He had conducted intellectual conversations and read stimulating books. Copernicus made his way back to northern Poland to start his career as a dedicated churchman. It was here that he served the Catholic Church, defended territory, treated patients, and formulated his heliocentric model. It was here he would spend the next thirty-plus years developing his world-shifting astronomical theories.

RULING THE ROOST

Before he settled in for the long haul as a canon in Frombork, Copernicus moved to the small town of Lidzbark in Warmia to help out his uncle Lucas. He performed his canon duties remotely, while serving as a personal secretary and physician to his uncle. Lucas Watzenrode held a powerful position as a bishop. As his assistant, Copernicus traveled with him, met important people such as kings and queens, and served as an adviser. He stayed by his uncle's side for seven years.

In 1510, Copernicus joined the chapter of canons in Frombork. This chapter consisted of sixteen canons, most of whom lived in the town. Frombork is in Warmia, which was part of the territory of Royal Prussia. The seaside town was home to around one thousand inhabitants. The main industry was fishing, as the edge of town nearly met up with the Baltic Sea.

Copernicus's day job as canon consisted of performing clerical duties such as attending and serving Mass twice daily. He also carried out non-church-related duties, including the performance of community governance responsibilities. Although Warmia was under the rule of the king of Poland, the canons governed the land and its people. They collected taxes, rents, and tithes (a percentage of earnings used to support the church) from the townspeople. Canons also administered the law.

Copernicus performed his clerical duties inside the impressive cathedral in Frombork. In 2004, his remains were discovered under one of the altars. They were reburied in the church in 2010.

They served as judges and appointed other officials such as mayors and fishing inspectors. Canons also ruled on who could get a license to brew beer or who could own weapons.

After several years as a canon, Copernicus shifted from his role as a chancellor, who handled the account-

ing books, to administrator of lands, who distributed lands to new tenants. Despite his busy schedule and many duties as a canon, Copernicus still found time to study the skies over Frombork.

NOTHING VENTURED, NOTHING GAINED

Copernicus and the canonry governed the land around Frombork, including a region about 40 miles (65 km) away called Olsztyn. Copernicus did such a phenomenal job that he was elected by his fellow canons as the administrator general of Olsztyn Castle. He held the position for five years, from 1516 to 1521. He was responsible for collecting rent payments and dues from the towns, which made up the biggest chunk of revenue for the canons. He also presided over hearings that concerned the transfer of land ownership, such as when a farmer had grown too old to care for the land. He would work to get the farm up and running again and help distribute livestock.

During Copernicus's administration at Olsztyn, another war broke out. Wanting to regain their lands and

The Castle of Warmian Bishops in Olsztyn was headquarters for the Bishops of Warmia. This is where Copernicus served as administrator general and defended the land from the Teutonic Knights.

political power, the Teutonic Knights deliberately defied the peace treaty that was signed in 1466. Many of the villages the knights once built and settled now belonged to others, including Olsztyn. The knights illegally inched their way around the Kingdom of Poland, torching cities, stealing horses, and taking over land. In 1520, they attacked Frombork and incinerated the entire town. Most of the homes were destroyed, with only the cathedral spared.

On January 16, 1521, the Teutonic Knights made their way to Olsztyn and demanded that the city surrender. Copernicus had prepared for such an attack. He had sent a letter to the king of Poland asking for military assistance. Unfortunately, the letter never made it to the king. The knights continued and broke through the castle's gate. But Copernicus would not give in; he was determined to protect the town of Olsztyn and its people. He calmly and bravely set about defending the town. He had managed to secure weapons and form a small army to keep the intruders at bay. The Teutonic Knights eventually retreated. Copernicus had saved the town of Olsztyn and its people.

BALANCING THE BOOKS

As a canon, Copernicus's many duties included economic and financial matters. He was familiar with how money was used, the value of a coin, and how it circulated in Poland. He wrote several papers and essays in an effort to reform the Prussian currency.

In the early sixteenth century, Poland was not completely unified. Although most towns had sworn allegiance to the king, communities wanted to use the money they had, which wasn't always Polish currency. This made for a very confusing exchange of goods. It would be like trying to use Monopoly money to buy a loaf of bread, and the baker saying she accepts only Candy Crush coins. It just doesn't work.

The problem started with how coins were made. Older coins were made of pure silver. But mints made newer coins by mixing melted-down silver coins with cheaper metals. The new coins were less valuable than the old coins. Copernicus recognized the problem. He discussed the tangled currency and recommended a solution in his treatise *Monete Cudende Ratio* (On the Minting of Coin). The title underwent several drafts and years of revision and thought. Copernicus was a stickler for accuracy and took his time before presenting and defending his ideas in public. The treatise suggested

Gold and silver coins were often minted with lesser-valued metals, such as copper. Copernicus believed that a coin's value should match the actual value of the material from which it was made.

getting rid of all the cheaper coins that were mixed with lesser-valued metals. He reaffirmed the idea that "bad money drives out good," also known as Gresham's law. Copernicus thought consumers would hoard the good money (pure silver coins) and spend the bad money (mixed-metal coins). Only the lesser-valued coin would be circulated, which would be bad for merchants, businesses, and trade. Copernicus suggested that mints reissue new coins, all made from the same metals, and put them into circulation at the same time. The king ignored his advice, but years later his ideas were adopted.

AN IMPERIAL PILL A DAY WILL KEEP THE TOOTH DECAY AWAY

Copernicus and his medical training were a sight for sore eyes in Frombork. The chapter did not have a doctor, so he was quickly put to work. He tended to his fellow canons and the people of Frombork. Doctor Copernicus, as he was referred to, worked every day in the Hospital of the Holy Spirit. He practiced general medicine but probably did nothing more than offer remedies for everyday ailments. He did not perform surgery or bloodletting, which was popular at that time. Copernicus probably consulted the many medical books that he had purchased during his time at the University of Padua.

Although Copernicus did not contribute a major medical breakthrough or perform miracles, he treated patients with some curious remedies. Scribbled in the margin of one of his medical books were ingredients for the prescription recipe called Imperial Pill. Made up of twenty assorted ingredients, such as ginger, cinnamon, and aloe syrup, the pill was a catchall remedy for several different ailments. It could be taken anytime, morning or evening, with or without food. The Imperial Pill treated a variety of things, such as gray hair, sour digestion, coughs, tooth decay, gas, and insomnia. Copernicus's standard treatment consisted of a mix of herbs and tonics and a lot of praying, in the hope that God would take care of the rest.

Copernicus went on to treat and tend to four consecutive bishops of Warmia. He was the doctor in the house. He treated his family, including his aging uncle and his brother, who was sick with a severe chronic disease, possibly leprosy. Andreas later died from the long-lasting infection in 1518. Copernicus also donated his services to the peasants of Warmia. In many portraits of him, he is depicted holding a lily of the valley. The white bell-shaped flower was a symbol of medical doctors.

Portrait of Copernicus holding lily of the valley. Although he never obtained a medical degree, Copernicus took the practice of medicine seriously.

REACHING FOR THE STARS

Copernicus was a well-respected doctor who tended to peasants and bishops alike. He was a leader during wartime and a champion of currency change. But his life's work was in the stars.

After a long day at the hospital or in court, he would come home to either of two observatories he had built, in Frombork and Olsztyn. Evidence of his astronomical work still lingers in Olsztyn. Faint outlines of a sketch that looks like a grid remain on a plaster wall of the observatory there. The grid worked as a sundial when an acutely positioned mirror reflected light onto the wall, and there he would etch the light's location. The reflective sundial traced the sun's daily and yearly paths of light. With this information, Copernicus determined when the equinox would happen.

Unfortunately, very little of his library has survived. Some of the books may have been auctioned, while others may have been burned or torn to shreds. But a few books have been found over the years. While studying astronomy at the University of Kraków, he had purchased *Tabulae Directionum* by Regiomontanus. This title was probably read with fervor, as Copernicus later added a sixteen-page appendix to his copy, with his own notes on astronomy and mathematics. His copy of

Ptolemy's *Geographia* (also known as *Geography* or *Cosmographia*) presented a coordinate grid for the latitude and longitude and the relationship between time and place within the heavens. Since his location was in the mostly cloudy Baltic Sea region, Copernicus used observations from ancient astronomers. Ptolemy's *Almagest* proved to be a great resource. Plus it had instructions for building basic astronomical instruments.

Copernicus used simple astronomical tools—some of which were probably handmade—including

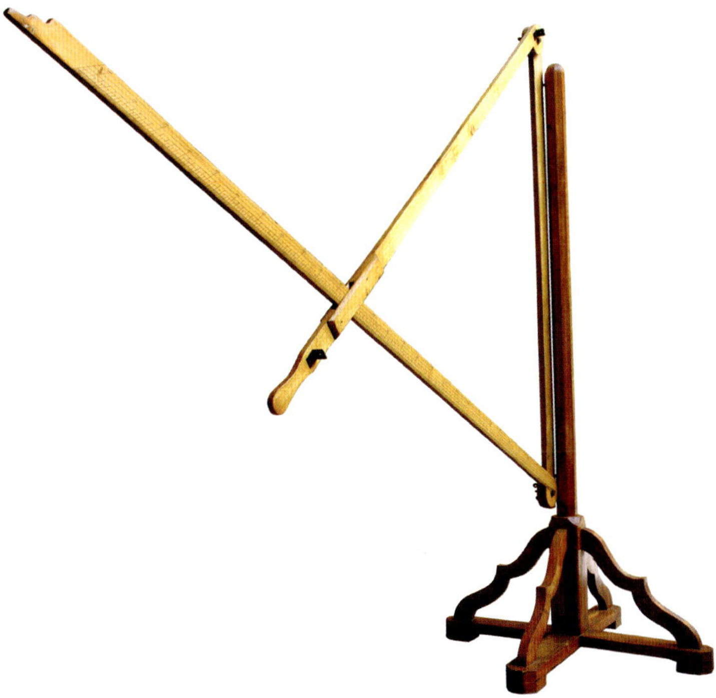

Copernicus used his homebuilt, eight-foot- (2.4-meter-) long triquetrum—what Ptolemy called a "parallactic instrument"—to measure the distance of the moon from Earth.

a wooden solar quadrant that was used for measuring the height of the sun over the horizon. He employed an astrolabe to calculate the position and latitude of celestial bodies. One of the only surviving instruments used by Copernicus is his triquetrum. Made of three pieces of wood angled together, it measured the angles of faraway objects, such as the moon, to determine their distance from Earth. This ancient instrument design was used by Ptolemy, Copernicus, and several astronomers after him, including Tycho Brahe.

SEEING INTO THE FUTURE

It's difficult to understand how Copernicus developed world-changing concepts using observations made with the naked eye. Imagine what he could have done with proper astronomical tools such as a telescope! But the telescope wasn't invented until much later. One of humankind's most important tools, the telescope gave people the ability to gain perspective of their place in the universe and check out things that had previously been too far away to see or even comprehend.

Although the telescope has helped scientists see the universe more clearly, the credit for the invention is muddled and often argued over by historians. The first person to lay claim to the device was a Dutch eyeglass maker named Hans Lippershey (or Lipperhey). In 1608, he applied for a patent covering a special eyepiece project. The design consisted of a convex lens and concave lens inside a tube. It allowed the viewer to see objects at three or four times their actual size. Some say that Lippershey pilfered the idea from another eyeglass maker in town, Zacharias Jansen. Both men invented optical instruments, but scholars say there is no real evidence that the design was stolen. Jansen is credited with the invention of the compound microscope, which is similarly built with two lenses in a tube—except it's used to magnify images of small, nearby objects. Compound microscopes are often found in modern high school science labs.

But Galileo Galilei was the first one who pointed a telescope toward the sky. He tinkered with the design and built his own with a higher magnifying power. With his amped-up telescope, Galileo observed multitudes of stars never seen before. He could see craters and mountains on the moon. He witnessed Venus going through phases and could see four moons of Jupiter. Galileo's telescope helped to confirm and support Copernicus's heliocentric model of the universe.

Because history is messy and disjointed, scholars and historians do their best to reimagine the past with the clues left behind with regard to what may have inspired Copernicus's innovative ideas and what motivated him.

MAN OF MYSTERY

Although Copernicus frequented the hospital and attended to civic matters, he was a loner. His friends from the university and his astronomy colleagues lived far away. He kept in touch through letters, but at home in Frombork, he mostly kept his private life private. However, he did get into trouble a few times.

During the sixteenth century, church canons were expected to take a vow of celibacy—to not marry and stay sexually abstinent. Most of the time, canons abided by the vow, but some ignored it, including Copernicus. But he wasn't the only one. Of the sixteen canons at Frombork, it is thought that three never took the vow and had intimate relationships.

The woman thought to have captured Copernicus's heart was Anna Schilling. She was a distant relative of his who had recently separated from her husband. She was pretty and well educated and also shared a love for gazing at the stars. Copernicus asked her to stay in his home as a housekeeper. It was common practice to hire relatives as housekeepers. But people thought there was more going on and felt that the arrangement was unfit for a Frombork canon. Copernicus was confronted and told to fire Schilling and kick her out. He agreed but did not follow through. Schilling stayed, and the bishop was informed. Letters were written about how to handle the defiance. When confronted again, Copernicus said he had dismissed Schilling and hadn't seen her since. After the controversy, Schilling was exiled from Frombork, never to return again. She may have gained the reputation of being a temptress and seducer. Often heroes of the past are placed high up on a pedestal, untouchable and perfect. However, they, too, are human with real stories, real problems, and real heartache.

CHAPTER FIVE

Bragging Rights

Copernicus was a true Renaissance man. He had been groomed for many skills, but his leading talent was astronomy. He spent years developing his ideas, yet he published only a few works. His final vita includes just three astronomical works: the *Commentariolus*, *Letter Against Werner*, and his masterpiece *De Revolutionibus*, which turned the world upside down, was banned by the church, and ultimately became the impetus for the Scientific Revolution.

THE *COMMENTARIOLUS*

It is difficult to extract the exact time period when Copernicus made his radical breakthrough. Like a lot of big ideas, it probably was not spurred from a single moment, but rather developed over time. Events, people, or even observations such seeing as a lunar eclipse may have inspired his innovation. But scholars believe that he began fiddling around with the heliocentric model of the universe sometime between 1508 and 1514.

The *Commentariolus* is what you might today call a sneak peek. Copernicus wrote about his heliocentric model for the first time in the short, concise manuscript, which was not released publicly. It was carefully circulated to just a few friends sometime around 1514. The *Commentariolus* contains only about forty pages. It

Created by Polish artist Jan Matejko, *Conversations with God* depicts Copernicus observing the night sky near his cathedral home in Frombork.

outlines seven assumptions or theories for his heliocentric model of the universe. Copernicus states that Earth and all the planets revolve around the sun. He explains that what appears to be retrograde motion is created by Earth's movement. He asserts that the moon revolves around Earth, and that Earth rotates on its own axis once every twenty-four hours. He also claims the universe is much larger than had been previously believed. He offers a correct (for the first time ever) order of the planets in the solar system, at least the ones that could be seen with the naked eye.

The *Commentariolus* was intended to be only an introduction to Copernicus's ideas, which he would later prove with mathematical demonstrations and observations. He writes in the manuscript that he purposely was brief, saving the rest for his larger work, *De Revolutionibus.* He sent the preview of his first book out to a few astronomers and philosophers. His work was reviewed well, except for a few critics who noted his heliocentric model appeared to disagree with church teachings. Copernicus was not deterred, though. He continued working on his masterpiece, not revealing it for another twenty or so years.

LETTER AGAINST WERNER

Copernicus was brilliant. He thought outside the box and challenged ideas, but perhaps he wasn't the best pen pal. *Letter Against Werner* was a belated response to his dear friend Bernard Wapowski. Once his classmate and roommate, Wapowski admired Copernicus's brilliance and asked for his thoughts on a recent work. He sent an essay titled *De Motu Octavae Sphaerae Tractatus Primus* (Letter Concerning the Motion of the Eighth Sphere), which was written by Johann Werner in 1522. Werner was a German mathematician and a priest at the Church of St. John in the city of Nuremberg. He also had an interest in astronomy and building astronomical instruments. You name it, he could build it. He built astrolabes, clocks, sundials, and more. He used these tools in an attempt to solve theoretical problems in spherical astronomy. According to Copernicus, Werner made fundamental contributions to trigonometry, but his astronomical work was subpar.

On June 3, 1524, Copernicus sat down to write his reply to Wapowski's request for evaluation of the widely praised essay. His unfiltered words were not kind. However, he likely did not imagine that others would read his response. In his letter, he criticized Werner for "defaming the ancients." He said Werner was deranged and foolish, but in the same breath stated that "it is one thing to snap at a man and assail him, but another thing to set him right and redirect him when he strays." Copernicus aimed to set Werner right by pointing out his mistakes. First he corrected

Although Copernicus never intended his *Letter Against Werner* to be made public, Wapowski considered its content too important not to share, especially the assertion that observation trumps theory.

the date Werner gave for Ptolemy's *Almagest*—Werner was eleven years off. He also claimed that Werner's ideas were based on theory, whereas ancient facts were based on observations. Copernicus stated that we must "hold fast to their observations, bequeathed like a legacy."

ALL ROADS LEAD TO ROME

For many years, dating back to the Middle Ages, the Roman Catholic Church held exclusive authority in all scientific and philosophical communication and education. The church was the law of the land and of the universe. The church endorsed and taught Ptolemy's model of the universe—one that employed Aristotle's prime mover, which the church identified as God. As the church gained popularity and power, it became difficult and dangerous for anyone to challenge its ideas and teachings. During the sixteenth century, religious leaders feared that heretics would spread ideas that contradicted the Bible and their stated truths. Scientists who declared opposing truths were publicly persecuted. The status and authority of the church likely influenced Copernicus's decision to publish or not to publish his manuscripts.

Toward the end of his letter, Copernicus stopped short of asserting his own opinion, writing, "Since [my views] are to be stated elsewhere, I deemed it superfluous and improper to extend this communication further here." This was clearly another teaser alluding to his larger masterpiece, *De Revolutionibus.*

MOVING HEAVEN AND EARTH

After decades of writing, Copernicus finally completed his opus. Scholars believe that he finished writing around 1530 but continued to revise and refine his work. Copernicus was not one to quickly push out ideas without having a solid foundation of evidence and consideration.

De Revolutionibus was four hundred pages, divided into six books and supplemented with elaborate geometric drawings and complicated astronomical tables. In the book, Copernicus outlines the assumptions made in *Commentariolus* and provides evidence for each. The first book of the major work, which is often considered the most important, delineates his heliocentric model of the universe. The model places a fixed sun at the center of the solar system and a spherical universe. Each planet moves in a perfect circle at a uniform speed. Because Copernicus chased a perfect ideal, his spherical motion still needed epicycles. The order of his planetary system placed Saturn

net, in quo terram cum orbe lunari tanquam epicyclo contineri diximus. Quinto loco Venus nono menſe reducitur. Sextum deniqꝫ locum Mercurius tenet, octuaginta dierum ſpacio circũ currens. In medio uero omnium reſidet Sol. Quis enim in hoc

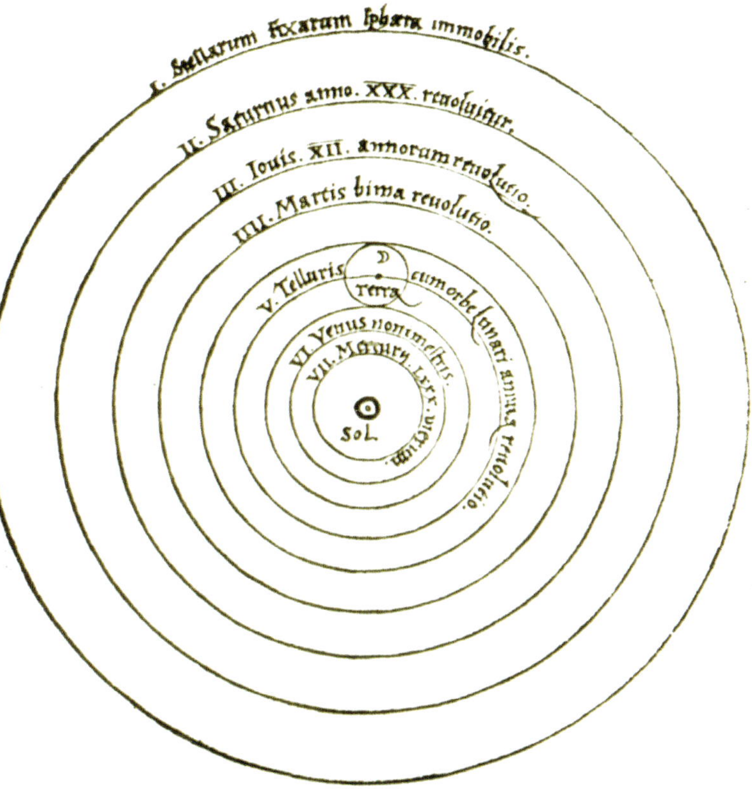

pulcherrimo templo lampadem hanc in alio uel meliori loco poneret, quàm unde totum ſimul poſsit illuminare? Siquidem non inepte quidam lucernam mundi, alij mentem, alij rectorem uocant. Trimegiſtus uiſibilem Deum, Sophoclis Electra intuentẽ omnia. Ita profecto tanquam in ſolio regali Sol reſidens circum agentem gubernat Aſtrorum familiam. Tellus quoqꝫ minime fraudatur lunari miniſterio, ſed ut Ariſtoteles de animalibus ait, maximã Luna cũ terra cognationẽ habet. Concipit interea à Sole terra, & impregnatur annuo partu. Inuenimus igitur ſub hac

A page from *De Revolutionibus* shows Copernicus's heliocentric diagram. He was the first to suggest an accurate order of the solar system. Notice that the orbits are not perfect circles, but ellipses.

farthest away, with a thirty-year orbit around the sun. Jupiter followed, with a twelve-year orbit. Next was Mars, with a two-year revolution, followed by Earth at one year. Venus's orbit came in at nine months, and Mercury, which held the sphere closest to the sun, had an eight-day orbit. His model established a planetary order with orbits in a unified system. The Copernican model proved to be much more accurate than Ptolemy's model, despite its imperfections.

The second book described the rotation and angle of Earth on its axis, which creates our day and night. Copernicus explained that Earth's movement is slow and natural, which is why an apple would fall straight to the ground and not fly off into outer space. As an added bonus, Copernicus offered step-by-step instructions to build an astrolabe.

Book three described how his model provided an accurate calendar of equinoxes and solstices. The fourth book delved into the moon's motions and lunar eclipses. Books five and six unraveled planetary longitude and latitude.

Some scholars have suggested that Copernicus was relentlessly chasing perfection. He longed to bring harmony to an overly complicated system. In *De Revolutionibus*, he wrote a dedicatory letter describing the disjointed geocentric theory:

> **...their experience was just like some one taking from various places hands, feet, a head, and other**

pieces, very well depicted, it may be, but not for the representation of a single person; since these fragments would not belong to one another at all, a monster rather than a man would be put together from them.

Copernicus may have been a perfectionist, but his aim was well placed. He took careful consideration when writing and revising his manuscript. His book's framework and design were intentional and logical. He was meticulous. He was thorough. Ruthlessly technical, *De Revolutionibus* contained hefty amounts of computations and calculations. Copernicus wanted to be taken seriously by scholars and his community of peers.

SLOW AND STEADY WINS THE RACE

Copernicus tirelessly worked on his masterpiece, yet he didn't have a publishing plan. Perhaps he was still tinkering with calculations or maybe he was nervous about the religious implications of his new model of the universe. Regardless of why he delayed publication, Copernicus was far away from a good sounding board to offer advice.

In the spring of 1539, a young German mathematician named Georg Joachim Rheticus traveled 433 miles (697 km) from Wittenberg, Germany, to Frombork. Rheticus was determined to meet the

Copernicus took careful consideration when writing and revising his manuscript to ensure accuracy. He offered tables of observations so that his peers could verify his research.

famed man who had dared to challenge popular belief. A professor of mathematics and astronomy at the University of Wittenberg, he had taken a leave from teaching in 1538 to tour the country, visiting famous scholars in astronomy and mathematics. It's unclear how Rheticus heard about Copernicus and his theories. Regardless of how and why, he showed up on Copernicus's doorstep in an attempt to persuade him to commit to publishing his manuscript, offering to help him add any finishing touches.

Rheticus's arrival offered the support and stimulating conversation that Copernicus needed for the final push. With the encouragement of his friends in the astronomical community, Copernicus finally went about publishing the full manuscript. He spent the next few years revising and cleaning up his pages. In the preface and dedication to Pope Paul III, Copernicus bravely states his heliocentric model, moving Earth from its God-given position in the center of the universe. But he also admits the fear of being "hooted off the stage drove me to almost abandon a work already undertaken."

While revising the work, Copernicus asked for advice from Andreas Osiander, a theologian and philosopher. He wondered if there was any way to minimize the potential backlash for publishing a manuscript that took a swing at the very core of church teachings. Osiander suggested introducing the book as a mere hypothesis, not claiming any sort of philosophical truth—essentially admitting that his ideas were just a mathematical theory and the results didn't matter. Copernicus completely disagreed. He rejected Osiander's idea and perhaps was insulted. He had spent a lifetime building his model, finding evidence to support it, and carefully presenting it in a way that would be comprehensible and respected by all readers. A hypothesis is an idea that may or not be true. But he believed his work was much more than that. It maintained both philosophical and mathematical truth.

However, Osiander had the last word. He was also the editor of the manuscript and oversaw its publication. He took advantage of his position and took it upon himself to offer an additional preface to the book. The one-page preface addressed the reader directly, stating, "if any causes are devised by the imagination, as indeed very many are, they are not put forward to convince anyone that they are true, but merely to provide a reliable basis for computation." Because the preface was unsigned, readers assumed Copernicus had written it.

Rheticus had secured the services of leading German printer Johannes Petreius, who had printed works by several well-known names, such as Martin Luther and Henry VII of England. Petreius's printing press was able and ready to print difficult academic texts with complex illustrations. In 1541, Copernicus

The German theologian Andreas Osiander not only added the unsigned preface falsely stating the work was a hypothesis, but he also changed the title of the book, adding "*orbium coelestium*."

finalized *De Revolutionibus* and the pages were sent off to Petreius.

A year before publication, Copernicus suffered a debilitating stroke. He was paralyzed and bedridden. *De Revolutionibus* was fresh from the printing press sometime in 1543. Some historians say that Copernicus died before viewing his publication, while others have said he finally received a copy on the day of his death. On May 24, 1543, at the age of seventy, Nicolaus Copernicus died from a brain hemorrhage, or stroke. Regardless of whether he saw the book or not, he was not around to witness the impact his publication was to make on the world.

CHAPTER SIX

Copernican Revolution

Copernicus was dead, but his words lived a lifetime and beyond. The printing and publication of *De Revolutionibus* made it available to anyone who could purchase and read it. The book was expensive, costing one florin (or ducat), which was equivalent to the price of one semester or term at a university. Only about four hundred copies were printed, which was the average number for a technical book. Although Copernicus knew his title might be a game changer, he wasn't so sure it would be a best seller.

FAILURE TO LAUNCH

The long-awaited manuscript had finally been published. Several people eagerly awaited the work's publication.

However, a few were completely distraught and upset after reading the first page. Tiedmann Giese, a dear friend who had tirelessly encouraged Copernicus to pursue his ideas and share them with the world, was utterly disappointed after reading the preface that Osiander had included in the book. Although the unsigned statement looked like it had been written by Copernicus, Giese knew the truth. He knew that his friend had not authored the words. He was irate and blamed the printer Petreius for the betrayal. Giese wrote a formal letter of complaint to the city council of Nuremberg, demanding that Petreius be held accountable and made to reprint a new and original untampered version. Petreius went to a formal hearing but was found innocent. Likewise, Rheticus also was shocked by the preface, but he knew where to point the finger. He had remembered Osiander's suggestion to Copernicus prior to sending the manuscript to him for editing. Osiander was the last to handle the book before Petreius printed the words.

Despite the bogus preface, *De Revolutionibus* didn't cause the mayhem that some had predicted. The book was complex and full of mathematical equations, observations, and diagrams. Because the text was crammed with calculations, astrologers ate up the planetary position data. Astronomical tables were soon published based on Copernicus's calculations. But his heliocentric model of the universe was mostly overlooked, perhaps because

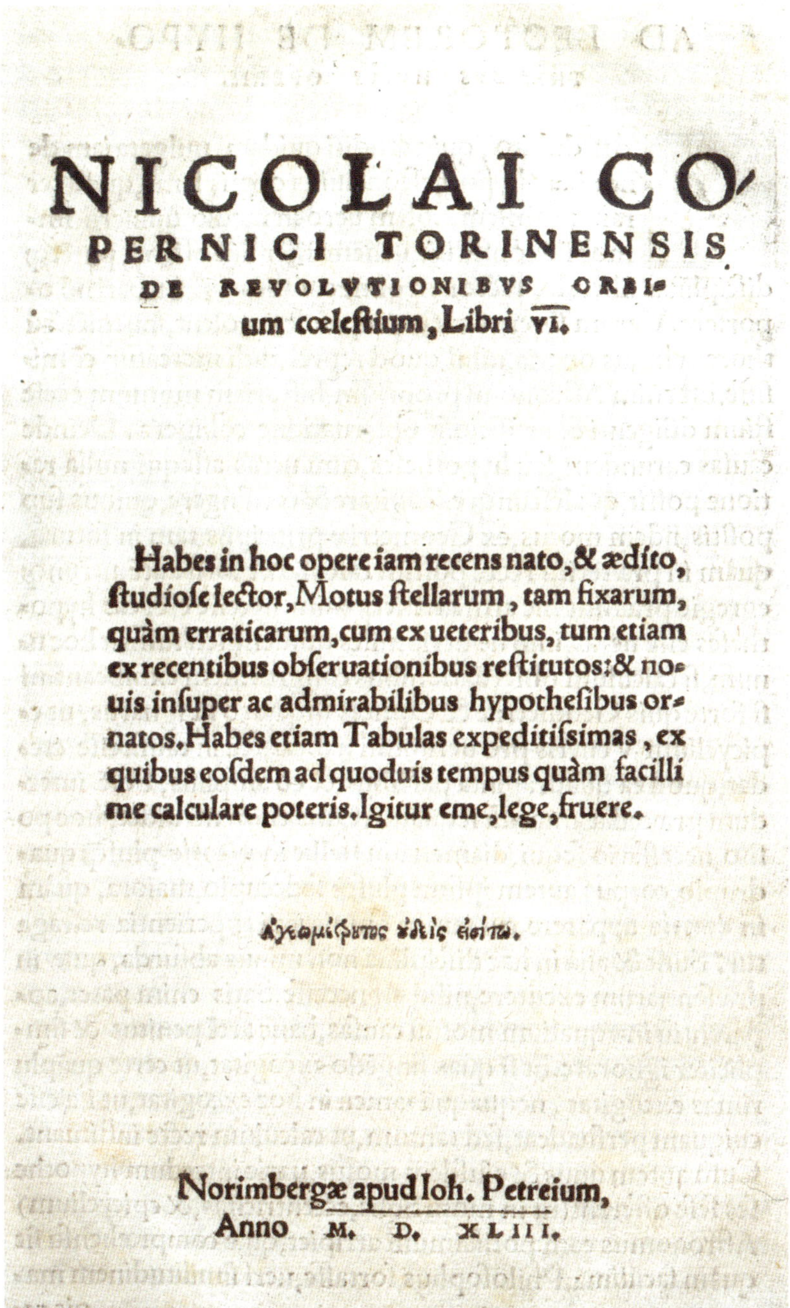

NICOLAI CO-
PERNICI TORINENSIS
DE REVOLVTIONIBVS ORBI-
um cœlestium, Libri VI.

Habes in hoc opere iam recens nato, & ædito, studiose lector, Motus stellarum, tam fixarum, quàm erraticarum, cum ex ueteribus, tum etiam ex recentibus obseruationibus restitutos: & nouis insuper ac admirabilibus hypothesibus ornatos. Habes etiam Tabulas expeditissimas, ex quibus eosdem ad quoduis tempus quàm facillime calculare poteris. Igitur eme, lege, fruere.

Ἀγεωμέτρητος οὐδεὶς εἰσίτω.

Norimbergæ apud Ioh. Petreium,
Anno M. D. XLIII.

On the title page of *De Revolutionibus,* the printer, Petreius, snuck in a marketing blurb introducing the text that essentially reminded readers to "buy, read, and enjoy the work."

GOD IS INFINITE, SO HIS UNIVERSE MUST BE, TOO

While Copernicus's *De Revolutionibus*, quietly laid in waiting for readership to develop, Giordano Bruno was shouting outrageous claims about the universe. An Italian philosopher and scientist, Bruno had an incredible memory. He became well known for his memory and was invited to Rome to show off his skills. But he was also very passionate and vocal about his philosophical ideas about the universe. He believed the universe was vast and boundless. He thought that if God was infinite, then his universe would also be infinite. Bruno proposed that other worlds like Earth existed, with intelligent beings. But most important, he was a champion of Copernicus's model. He advocated for a heliocentric system but thought there was not a true center of the universe.

Bruno was loved and hated. Because of his heretical words, he had quickly gained a reputation. He hopped around Europe, from Paris to Germany, England and Rome, evading the authorities. In 1592, he was finally arrested in Venice and sent to Rome for trial before the Roman Inquisition, a system officials organized to maintain and defend the integrity of the Catholic faith. Bruno was charged with a total of 130 counts, ranging from heretical outbursts to the possession of forbidden books. An eight-year trial followed in which he denied all charges except his philosophical ideas—including Copernican beliefs. In 1600, Bruno was found guilty of heresy and burned at the stake.

of Osiander's preface or because the text was very technical. It wasn't until 1616, more than seventy years after publication, that *De Revolutionibus* made the Catholic Church's Index of Forbidden Books.

BIRDS OF A FEATHER

In the decades following Copernicus's death, a few scholars started reading his words, and they wanted more. Inspired by Copernicus's model, scientists began to further explore this notion that Earth was not at the center of everything.

Tycho Brahe of Denmark was born just three years after Copernicus died. The oldest of eleven kids, he wore a golden nosepiece after his nose was sliced off in a swordfight during his university days. He was a lover of astronomy and astrology. He purchased books and instruments on these subjects, and he studied the

Although Tycho didn't fully accept Copernicus's heliocentric model, when he received Copernicus's triquetrum while visiting Frombork, he was moved to compose a poem in honor of Copernicus and the tool.

heavens nightly. In 1572, he observed a supernova and watched it carefully for several months. He determined that it wasn't a comet, as most thought, but was instead a fixed star. Tycho was extremely ambitious. He persuaded the king of Denmark to build him an observatory filled with all the best and most advanced astronomical instruments available. He was also a huge fan of Copernicus and his work, although he never totally accepted the latter's heliocentric model of the universe. But he diligently read the *Commentariolus* and even acquired Copernicus's triquetrum, which he cherished.

From his observations and astronomical measurements, Tycho developed his own model of the universe called the Tyconic system. It was a fusion of Ptolemy's and Copernicus's models. Earth was still at the center, but Mercury, Venus, Mars, Jupiter, and Saturn all revolved around the sun. And the sun, moon, and stars revolved around Earth.

His research assistant, Johannes Kepler, had different ideas. Kepler was a brilliant mathematician whom Tycho had hired to analyze data. When Tycho died unexpectedly, Kepler inherited his notebooks and continued the astronomical work. But unlike Tycho, Kepler preferred and often defended Copernicus's heliocentric model over Ptolemy's geocentric model. He worked toward proving the sun was the center of the universe. Kepler concluded that Earth and the other planets orbited the sun, but

Using Tycho's observational data, Kepler formulated three laws of planetary motion, including the elliptical orbits. Later Isaac Newton used Kepler's laws to validate his law of gravity.

not in the perfectly ordered and shaped spheres of the Copernican model. Instead, he proposed that their orbits were eclipses. He published his insights on Copernicus's model in *Epitome Astronomiae Copernicanae* (*Epitome of Copernican Astronomy*). His work was divided into three volumes, which were published between 1617 and 1621. His title became a classic and was later studied and used by Isaac Newton.

PROOF IS IN THE PUDDING

Galileo Galilei was the one who sealed the deal and confirmed the Copernican model. Unfortunately, he also bore the brunt of the backlash that Copernicus might have endured himself had he lived beyond his publication date.

Galileo was an Italian philosopher, mathematician, and astronomer. He'd read and accepted Copernicus's theory and had even compiled his own data to support a heliocentric model. But he worried about the repercussions of announcing his work. He saw the ridicule and condemnation heaped upon *De Revolutionibus.* He wrote in a letter to Kepler, "I have collected many proofs, but I do not publish them, because I am deterred by the fate of our teacher Copernicus who, although he had won immortal fame with a few, was ridiculed and condemned by countless people." By this time,

Galileo was eventually forced to renounce the heliocentric model to avoid being burned at the stake. More than 350 years later, the Catholic Church acknowledged its mistake.

De Revolutionibus had made the Catholic Church's Index of Banned Books. Pope Urban VII said that the book could cause more damage than the opposition growing within the Protestant movement.

After observations with the telescope and further research, Galileo couldn't stay silent any longer. He published several works about his findings, including his famous *Dialogo sopra i Due Massimi Sistemi del Mondo, Tolemaico e Copernicano* (*Dialogue Concerning the Two Chief World Systems, Ptolemaic and Copernican*), published in 1632. The title referred to a fictitious conversation between three scholars. One scholar firmly believed in Ptolemy's geocentric model, while the other believed in Copernicus's heliocentric model. The third scholar remained neutral, listening to both sides as they attempted to prove and persuade the listener of their truth. The book was popular, perhaps because it was readable and relatable. However, the clever story brought trouble. In 1633, Galileo was ordered to defend himself and his work in front of the Roman Inquisition. He was found guilty of teaching and

Isaac Newton's biographer William Stukeley reported that Newton did sit under a tree contemplating why falling apples did not go sideways. Unlike the stories indicate, though, an apple never fell on his head.

defending Copernicus's outlawed beliefs. Galileo was sentenced to live the rest of his days under house arrest. But the Copernican model continued to thrive with Galileo's observations and his strong advocacy.

Years later, Isaac Newton placed the icing on the Copernican cake. Newton gave evidence of universal gravity that explained why the planets orbit the sun and why moons orbit their home planets. His prime example supposedly involved an apple falling from the tree directly to the ground.

IT'S ALL JUST SPACE DUST

Little did the unassuming church canon with an affinity for perfect circles know that his title *De Revolutionibus* would be a powerful catalyst for the Scientific Revolution. Innovation is born from a deep-rooted curiosity and the courage to ask questions. Copernicus bravely turned the world

The bronze statue of Copernicus stands in the main square in Toruń, Poland. The monument's inscription reads, "Nicolaus Copernicus of Toruń, moved the Earth, held the Sun and the heavens."

upside down and inspired those who followed him to do the same. Without Tycho's ambition and nightly sky watch, Kepler's brilliant mathematical mind wouldn't have had the observational data to crunch. Kepler's diligence passed the torch to Galileo. Without Galileo's curious eye pointed toward the sky, and his perseverance and conviction to get the word out, Copernicus's publication might have continued to gather space dust. As Isaac Newton once stated, "If I have seen further, it is by standing upon the shoulders of giants." The light of discovery shines bright on many.

Timeline

1473 Nicolaus Copernicus is born on February 19 in Toruń, Poland.

1483 Copernicus's father dies.

1491 Attends the University of Kraków to study astronomy.

1496 Attends the University of Bologna to study canon law. He meets Domenico Maria Novara and makes his first recorded astronomical observations.

1500 Spends the Jubilee year in Rome; gives public lectures on mathematics.

1501 Attends the University of Padua to study medicine.

1503 Awarded a doctorate in canon law from the University of Ferrara. He returns to Poland and serves as a personal assistant and physician to his uncle Lucas in Lidzbark, Poland.

1510 Leaves his uncle to join the chapter of canons in Frombork, Poland.

1520 War breaks out between the Kingdom of Poland and the Teutonic Knights.

1521 Successfully defends the land against the Teutonic Knights.

1524 Writes his *Letter Against Werner*, a letter to Bernard Wapowski criticizing the views of astronomer Johann Werner.

1526 Writes the essay *Monete Cudende Ratio* on reforming Prussian currency.

1539 Mathematician Georg Joachim Rheticus visits Copernicus, encouraging him and supporting Copernicus in the publication of his manuscript *De Revolutionibus.*

1541 Finishes *De Revolutionibus*, after many revisions, and sends his manuscript to be printed.

1543 *De Revolutionibus* is published in Nuremberg, Germany. Copernicus dies on May 24 in Frombork and is buried in the local cathedral.

GLOSSARY

ARMILLARY SPHERE A movable model of the celestial globe with rings and hoops representing the different celestial spheres.

ASTROLABE An astronomical instrument used to calculate the position and latitude of celestial bodies.

ASTROLOGY The study of the movements of celestial bodies and phenomena and their interpreted influence on humans and events.

ASTRONOMY The study of planets, stars, and other celestial bodies and phenomena.

CANON An appointed church official who carries out the business of the church.

CANON LAW The official laws made by the Catholic Church for the government of the church and its members.

CARTOGRAPHER A person who makes maps or charts.

DEFERENT The main sphere on which planets orbited around Earth in the Ptolemaic model of the universe.

EPICYCLE A smaller sphere on which a planet orbited around a point on the deferent in the Ptolemaic model of the universe.

EQUINOX When the sun passes directly over the earth's equator, and the day and night are of equal length. It happens twice a year.

GEOCENTRIC Referring to an Earth-centered model of the universe.

GRESHAM'S LAW An economic theory that states lower valued money drives out higher valued money.

HELIOCENTRIC Referring to a sun-centered model of the universe.

HERETIC Someone who doesn't accept the standard beliefs of a religion.

HOROSCOPE A prediction of future events based on the positions of stars and planets at the time of a person's birth.

HUMORAL THEORY An ancient Greek medical theory that said the body is made up four humors: blood, phlegm, yellow bile, and black bile.

NATIONALITY Identifying or belonging to a particular country or nation.

OCCAM'S RAZOR The principle that the simplest explanation is often the best.

OCCULTATION When one celestial body passes in front of another.

PAGAN A person who practices a religion other than popular world religion, such as Christianity.

PRIME MOVER The creator of movement in the universe, according to Aristotle.

PRINTING PRESS A machine used for printing books.

RETROGRADE MOTION An illusion of backward motion that is created when Earth's orbit passes slower moving outer planets.

SOLAR QUADRANT An astronomical instrument used for measuring the height of the sun over the horizon.

SOLSTICE When the sun is at the greatest distance from the celestial equator, creating the longest and shortest days of the year.

SUNDIAL An astronomical instrument that measures the time of day by the position of the sun and sunlight.

TRIQUETRUM An astronomical instrument used to measure angles of faraway objects, such as stars, to determine distance.

For More Information

American Astronomical Society
1667 K Street NW, Suite 800
Washington, DC 20006
(202) 328-2010
Website: https://aas.org
The American Astronomical Society's mission is to enhance and share humanity's scientific understanding of the universe.

Canadian Astronomical Society
100 Viaduct Avenue W
Victoria, BC V9E 1J3
Canada
(301) 675-8957
Website: http://casca.ca
The Canadian Astronomical Society is devoted to the advancement of knowledge of the universe though research and education.

International Astronomical Union
IAU–UAI Secretariat
98-bis Blvd Arago
F–75014 Paris
France
Website: http://www.iau.org

The International Astronomical Union promotes and safegaurds the science of astronomy through international cooperation.

Nicolaus Copernicus Museum
Katedralna 8
14-530 Frombork
Poland
Website: http://frombork.art.pl/pl
The Nicolaus Copernicus Museum is dedicated to the life and work of Copernicus and is located in Frombork, Poland, where he spent his working years.

The Planetary Society
60 South Los Robles Avenue
Pasadena, CA 91101
(626) 793-5100
Website: http://www.planetary.org
The Planetary Society is dedicated to supporting innovative space technologies and nurturing creative young minds.

Royal Astronomical Society of Canada
203-4920 Dundas Street W
Toronto, ON M9A 1B7

Canada
(416) 924-7973
Website: http://www.rasc.ca
The Royal Astronomical Society of Canada is a non-profit organization dedicated to the advancement of astronomy. It has local branches, called centres, across Canada.

Universities Space Research Association
7178 Columbia Gateway Drive
Columbia, MD 21046
(410) 730-2656
Website: http://www.usra.edu
The Universities Space Research Association is a non-profit research corporation devoted to the advancement of space science and technology.

WEBSITES

Because of the changing nature of internet links, Rosen Publishing has developed an online list of websites related to the subject of this book. This site is updated regularly. Please use this link to access the list:

http://www.rosenlinks.com/LOSR/copernicus

For Further Reading

Barber, Nicola. *Renaissance Medicine* (Medicine Through the Ages). North Mankato, MN: Heinemann-Raintree Library, 2012.

Bell, Jim. *The Space Book: From the Beginning to the End of Time, 250 Milestones in the History of Space and Astronomy.* New York, NY: Sterling Publishing Company Incorporated, 2013.

Bortz, Fred. *The Sun-Centered Universe and Nicolaus Copernicus* (Revolutionary Discoveries of Scientific Pioneers). New York, NY: Rosen Publishing, 2013.

Curley, Robert. *Scientists and Inventors of the Renaissance.* New York, NY: Rosen Publishing, 2012.

Faulk, Richard. *The Next Big Thing: A History of the Boom-or-Bust Moments That Shaped the Modern World.* Boston, MA: Houghton Mifflin Harcourt, 2015.

Gardner, Robert. *Astronomy Experiments in Your Own Observatory* (Design, Build, Experiment). New York, NY: Enslow Publishers, 2015.

Gilliland, Ben. *Rocket Science for the Rest of Us.* London, UK: DK Publishing, 2015.

Grant, John. *Eureka! 50 Scientists Who Shaped Human History.* Boston, MA: Houghton Mifflin Harcourt, 2016.

Marcovitz, Hal. *Life During the Renaissance* (Living

History). San Diego, CA: ReferencePoint Press, 2015.

McKenna, Amy. *Estonia, Latvia, Lithuania, and Poland* (The Britannica Guide to Countries of the European Union). New York, NY: Rosen Publishing, 2013.

Miller, Ron. *Recentering the Universe: The Radical Theories of Copernicus, Kepler, Galileo, and Newton.* Minneapolis, MN: Lerner Publishing Group, 2013.

Roscoe, Kelly, and Mick Isle. *Aristotle: The Father of Logic* (Greatest Greek Philosophers). New York, NY: Rosen Publishing, 2015.

Bibliography

Andronik, Catherine M. *Copernicus: Founder of Modern Astronomy* (Great Minds of Science). New York, NY: Enslow Publishers, 2009.

Barker, Peter. "Copernicus and the Critics of Ptolemy." *Journal for the History of Astronomy* 11, 1999.

Bogdanowicza, Wiesław, et al. "Genetic Identification of Putative Remains of the Famous Astronomer Nicolaus Copernicus." *Proceedings of the National Academy of Sciences* 106, no. 30, 2009.

Copernican Academic Portal. "Nicolaus Copernicus Thorunensis." Nicolaus Copernicus University in Toru , the City of Toru and the Institute for the History of Science, Polish Academy of Sciences. February 19, 2010. http://copernicus.torun.pl/en.

Gingerich, Owen. *The Book Nobody Read: Chasing the Revolutions of Nicolaus Copernicus.* London, UK: Bloomsbury Publishing, 2009.

Gingerich, Owen. "The Copernicus Grave Mystery." *Proceedings of the National Academy of Sciences* 106, no. 30, 2009.

Harvard University Library. "Contagion Historical Views of Diseases and Epidemics: Humoral Theory." Retrieved September 11, 2016. http://ocp.hul .harvard.edu/contagion/humoraltheory.html.

Hawking, Stephen W. *On the Shoulders of Giants: The*

Great Works of Physics and Astronomy. Philadelphia, PA: Running Press, 2003.

Repcheck, Jack. *Copernicus' Secret: How the Scientific Revolution Began*. New York, NY: Simon and Schuster, 2007.

Rosen, Edward. *Copernicus and the Scientific Revolution*. Malabar, FL: Krieger, 1984.

Rutkowski, Boleslaw, et al. "Nicolaus Copernicus: Not Only a Great Astronomer but Also a Physician." *American Journal of Nephrology* 17, 2011.

Sakolsky, Josh. *Copernicus and Modern Astronomy*. New York, NY: Rosen Publishing, 2005.

Samuels, Charlie. *Timeline of the Renaissance* (History Highlights). New York, NY: Gareth Stevens, 2010.

Swerdlow, Noel M. "The Derivation and First Draft of Copernicus's Planetary Theory: A Translation of the Commentariolus with Commentary." *Proceedings of the American Philosophical Society* 117.6, 1973.

Van Helden, Albert. "Giordano Bruno (1548-1600)." The Galileo Project, Rice University, 1995. http://galileo.rice.edu/chr/bruno.html.

Westman, Robert. *The Copernican Question: Prognostication, Skepticism, and Celestial Order*. Oakland, CA: University of California Press, 2011.

INDEX

A

Almagest, 15, 17, 19, 61, 69, 71
almanac, astrological, 43
Aristarchus, 12, 13
Aristotle, 8–10, 11, 38, 71
armillary sphere, 38
astrolabes, 38, 41, 62, 69, 74
astrologers, 18, 40, 41, 82
astrology, 38, 40, 41, 45, 85
astronomers, 4, 18, 28, 38, 40, 61, 62, 68, 89
  European, 15
  Greek, 11
  life of, 8
  observational, 18
astronomical tables, 18, 72, 82
astronomy, 20, 38, 40, 41, 43, 50, 64, 66, 69, 77, 85
  ancient, 15
  concepts of, 15
  Copernicus as founder of modern, 4, 28
  European, 18
  medical, 44
  school of, 37, 38, 41, 43, 60, 77
  spherical, 69
  theoretical, 40
  tools of, 20, 38, 61–62, 69, 87
works of, 20, 28, 33, 50, 60, 66, 69, 87

B

Bruno, Giordano, 84, 85

C

canon, 4, 33, 43, 44, 49, 51, 52–53, 55, 57, 64–65, 93
canon law, 42–43, 49, 50
cartographer, 37–38
childhood, of Copernicus, 23–25, 33
Commentariolus, 66–68, 72, 87
currency, Copernicus's ideas to reform, 4, 34, 55, 56, 60

D

deferent, 13, 15
De Revolutionibus Orbium Coelestium (*On the Revolutions of the Heavenly Spheres*), 6, 13, 43, 66, 68, 72, 74–75, 78, 80, 81, 82, 84, 85, 89, 91, 93

Dialogo sopra i Due Massimi Sistemi del Mondo, Tolemaico e Copernicano (*Dialogue Concerning the Two Chief World Systems, Ptolemaic and Copernican*), 91
doctor, 4, 8, 57, 58, 60
  Copernicus studies to be, 44–45, 47, 49

E

eclipse, lunar, 9, 38, 43–44, 67, 74, 89
epicycle, 15, 72
Epitome (*Epytoma Joannis de Monte Regio in Almagestum Ptolomei*), 19, 40
Epitome Astronomiae Copernicanae (*Epitome of Copernican Astronomy*), 89
equinox, 18, 60, 74

G

Galen, 45
Galileo Galilei, 6, 63, 89, 91, 93, 95
geocentric model of the universe, 4, 6, 9, 11, 17, 38, 41, 74–75, 87, 91
Geographia, 60–61
Giese, Tiedmann, 82
God
  in Bruno's theories, 84–85
  as creator of universe, 77
  as prime mover, 11, 71
  role in medicine, 58
gravity, 9–10, 93
Gresham's law, 57
Gutenberg, Johannes, 31

H

heliocentric model of the universe, 12, 13, 50, 63, 67–68, 72, 77, 82, 84, 85, 87, 89, 91
heretics, 71, 84, 85
Hippocrates, 45
horoscopes, 40, 44–45
humoral theory, 45, 47

I

Imperial Pill, 57–58
Inquisition, Roman, 84–85, 91

J

Jubilee, 43

K

Kepler, Johannes, 6, 87, 89, 95

L

Letter Against Werner, 66, 68–69, 71

M

Mathematike Syntaxis (*The Mathematical Arrangement*), 15
Middle Ages, 6, 71
Monete Cudende Ratio (*On the Minting of Coin*), 56

N

name, of Copernicus, 28, 30
nationalism, 30
nationality, of Copernicus, 28, 30
Newton, Isaac, 89, 93, 95
Novara, Domenico Maria, 43

O

observatories, 20, 38, 60
Occam's razor, 17
occultation, 43
Osiander, Andreas, 77–78, 82, 85

P

pagans, 27
Petreius, Johannes, 78, 80, 82
Peuerbach, Georg von, 18, 19, 20, 38
Plato, 9
prime mover, 9–10, 11, 71
printing press, 20, 31, 33, 78, 80
Ptolemy, Claudius, 11, 13, 15, 19, 38, 60–61, 62, 69, 71, 74, 87, 91
  model of the universe, 17

R

Regiomontanus (Johann Müller von Königsberg), 18, 19, 20, 38, 40, 60
Renaissance, 4, 30, 66
retrograde motion, 13, 15, 68
Rheticus, Georg Joachim, 75, 77, 78, 82

S

solar quadrant, 61–62
solstices, 74
sundial, 60, 69
supernova
  Copernicus as, 4, 6

observation of, 87

T

Tabulae Directionum (*Tables of Directions*), 19
telescope, invention of, 62–63, 91
Teutonic Knights, 4, 25, 26–27, 28, 30, 54–55
Toruń, Poland, 23, 24, 25, 26–28, 34, 35
trigonometry, 19–20, 69
triquetrum, 62, 87
Tycho Brahe, 85, 87, 89

U

University of Bologna, 42
University of Ferrara, 49
University of Kraków, 36, 60
University of Padua, 44, 47, 49, 57

W

Wapowski, Bernard, 37–38, 69
Watzenrode, Lucas (Uncle Lucas), 33, 36, 42, 43, 44, 51

ABOUT THE AUTHOR

Kristina Lyn Heitkamp is a Montana-based author, researcher, and environmental journalist. She earned a bachelor of arts in English from the University of Utah and a master of arts in environmental science and natural resource journalism from the University of Montana. She is a researcher for National Geographic Books and a regular contributor to the children's science magazine *Muse*. While researching this book, Heitkamp rekindled her love for stargazing. In the same vein as Tycho Brahe, she has taken to a nightly sky watch and hopes to be around to witness comet Halley's return in the year 2061.

PHOTO CREDITS

Cover, p. 1 (portrait) Imagno/Hulton Archive/Getty Images; cover, p. 1 (background) Mansell/The LIFE Picture Collection/Getty Images; pp. 5, 10 Universal Images Group/Getty Images; p. 14 Leemage/Corbis Historical/Getty Images; pp. 16, 21, 48, 83 Science and Society Picture Library/Getty Images; pp. 19, 70 Pictorial Press Ltd/Alamy Stock Photo; p. 24 Culture Club/Hulton Archive/Getty Images; pp. 26–27, 79 Print Collector/Hulton Archive/Getty Images; pp. 29, 32–33 Bettmann/Getty Images; p. 37 Piero M. Bianchi/Moment/Getty Images; p. 39 Jeffrey Coolidge/Photodisc/Getty Images; p. 42 Interfoto/Alamy Stock Photo; p. 46 NYPL/Science Source/Getty Images; pp. 52–53 cobalt88/Shutterstock.com; p. 54 Martyn Jandula/Shutterstock.com; p. 56 Fedor Selivanov/Alamy Stock Photo; p. 59 Stock Montage/Archive Photos/Getty Images; p. 61 pryzmat/Shutterstock.com; p. 67 Andreas Ehrhard/Alamy Stock Photo; pp. 73, 90–91 Science Source/Getty Images; p. 76 National Geographic Creative/Bridgeman Images; p. 86 Kean Collection/Hulton Fine Art Collection/Getty Images; p. 88 Imagno/Hulton Fine Art Collection/Getty Images; pp. 92–93 Hulton Archive/Getty Images; p. 94 Teresa Kasprzycka/Shutterstock.com; back cover, pp. 8, 23, 36, 50, 66, 81 agsandrew/Shutterstock.com; interior pages background Ilya Bolotov/Shutterstock.com.

Designer: Brian Garvey; Editor: Amelie von Zumbusch; Photo Researcher: Karen Huang